Write 4 Today

Grade 5

Frank Schaffer Publications®

Editor: Linda Triemstra
Interior Designer: Lori Kibbey

Frank Schaffer Publications®

Send all inquiries to:
Frank Schaffer Publications
3195 Wilson Drive NW
Grand Rapids, Michigan 49534

Write 4 Today—grade 5

ISBN: 0-7682-3225-2

2 3 4 5 6 7 8 9 10 PAT 10 09 08 07 06 05

Write 4 Today

Table of Contents

Introduction....4

Writing Strategies....6

Graphic Organizers....7

Editing Checklist....12

Practice/Assessments....13

Answer Key....93

Introduction

Write 4 Today is a comprehensive yet quick and easy-to-use supplement sequenced to complement any fifth-grade writing curriculum. Essential writing skills and concepts are reviewed each day during a four-day period (Monday through Thursday) with an evaluation each fifth day (Friday).

Unlike many writing programs, *Write 4 Today* is designed on a continuous spiral so that concepts are repeated weekly. This book supplies four concepts for four days covering a forty-week period. The focus alternates weekly between the mechanics of writing (capitalization, grammar, punctuation, and spelling) and the process of writing (prewriting/brainstorming, drafting, revising, and proofreading). A separate assessment is provided for the fifth day of each week.

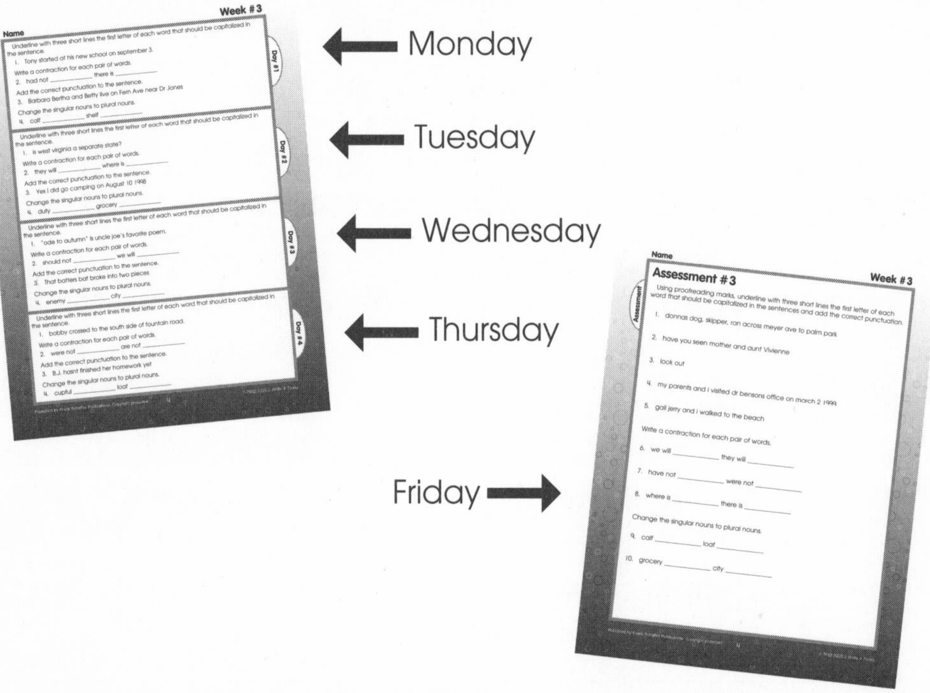

Because writing typically involves lengthier work than these short exercises require, many of the process exercises are ideal to use as springboards for more in-depth work. For example, if one task is creating an opening paragraph on a specific topic, the exercise could be expanded to include writing supporting paragraphs and a conclusion. A list of writing strategies, graphic organizers, and an editing checklist help students to hone their skills.

Answer keys are provided for daily drills and assessments (see pages 93–112). Concepts and skills are tested on an even/odd week rotation and follow a consistent format for ease of evaluation. Although the concepts and skills are individually categorized, most are interrelated so that many opportunities for practice and evaluation exist.

Write 4 Today was created in response to a need for ongoing practice after a skill had been addressed in the basal text. With the usual methods, a skill would be covered and then abandoned until it reappeared (sometimes) in a six-week cumulative review. With the growing emphasis on standardized testing, the necessity for experience with test styles and semantics also became apparent.

The daily approach of *Write 4 Today* provides risk-taking challenges, higher-level thinking exercises, problem-solving strategies, and necessary drill, emphasizing areas that frequently give students difficulty, such as punctuation and spelling. The program targets test-taking skills by incorporating the style and syntax of standardized tests.

For the even weeks, when the focus is on the writing process, use this ten-point rubic to assess the published work. You may cut and copy it onto the bottom of each assessment or attach it as a separate page. The rubic has been structured with a total of 10 possible points for each of the writing trait categories. These trait categories correlate with the popular 6 + 1 TRAITS* Writing Program (*a trademark of Northwest Regional Educational Laboratory) in this order from top to bottom: ideas, organization, voice, word choice, sentence fluency, conventions (covering all four COPS lines), and presentation. Use the rubic for student self assessments, or teacher assessments. Score the writing according to how often it clearly demonstrates each trait.

Never	Sometimes	Mostly	Always	**Grading Rubric**	
1	4	7	10	**Focus**	Writing sticks to the topic with focused main ideas and supporting details
1	4	7	10	**Order**	Sentences and paragraphs have a clear order that makes sense to readers
1	4	7	10	**Tone**	Words and sentences use an interesting tone of voice that fits the audience and the writing style
1	4	7	10	**Vocabulary**	Writing uses a wide variety of vocabulary that is specific, accurate, strong, and original
1	4	7	10	**Flow**	Sentences are easy to read and flow smoothly from one to the next
1	4	7	10	**Details**	Capitalization is correct
1	4	7	10		Odd Grammar is corrected before publishing
1	4	7	10		Punctuation is correct
1	4	7	10		Spelling is correct
1	4	7	10	**Neatness**	Writing is neat, clean, and easy to read

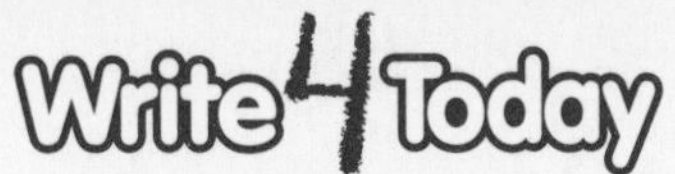

Writing Strategies

Choose a **topic** for your writing.
- What am I writing about?

Decide on a **purpose** for writing.
- Why am I writing this piece?
- What do I hope the audience will learn from reading this piece?

Identify your **audience**.
- Who am I writing to?

Decide on a writing **style**.
- Expository—gives information or explains facts or ideas
- Persuasive—tries to convince, to talk someone into something
- Narrative—tells a story
- Descriptive—presents a clear picture of a person, place, thing, or idea

Decide on a **genre**—essay, letter, poetry, autobiography, fiction, nonfiction.

Decide on a **point of view**—first person, second person, or third person.

Brainstorm by listing or drawing your main ideas.

Use a graphic organizer to organize your thoughts.

Revise, revise, revise!
- Use **descriptive words**.
- Use **transitions** and linking expressions.
- Use a **variety of sentence structures**.
- **Elaborate** with facts and details.
- Group your ideas into **paragraphs**.
- **Proofread** for capitalization, punctuation, and spelling.

Clustering Planner

Clustering is a kind of graphic planner used to brainstorm ideas, images, and feelings around a specific word or concept.

How It Works: When clustering, you begin with a word, concept, topic, or question and work outward, linking and recording thoughts using text or pictures. As thoughts tumble out, you expand your ideas from the center like branches on a tree. When one branch stops or if an idea doesn't fit, create a new branch. Brainstorming clusters are free-flowing and can take any shape.

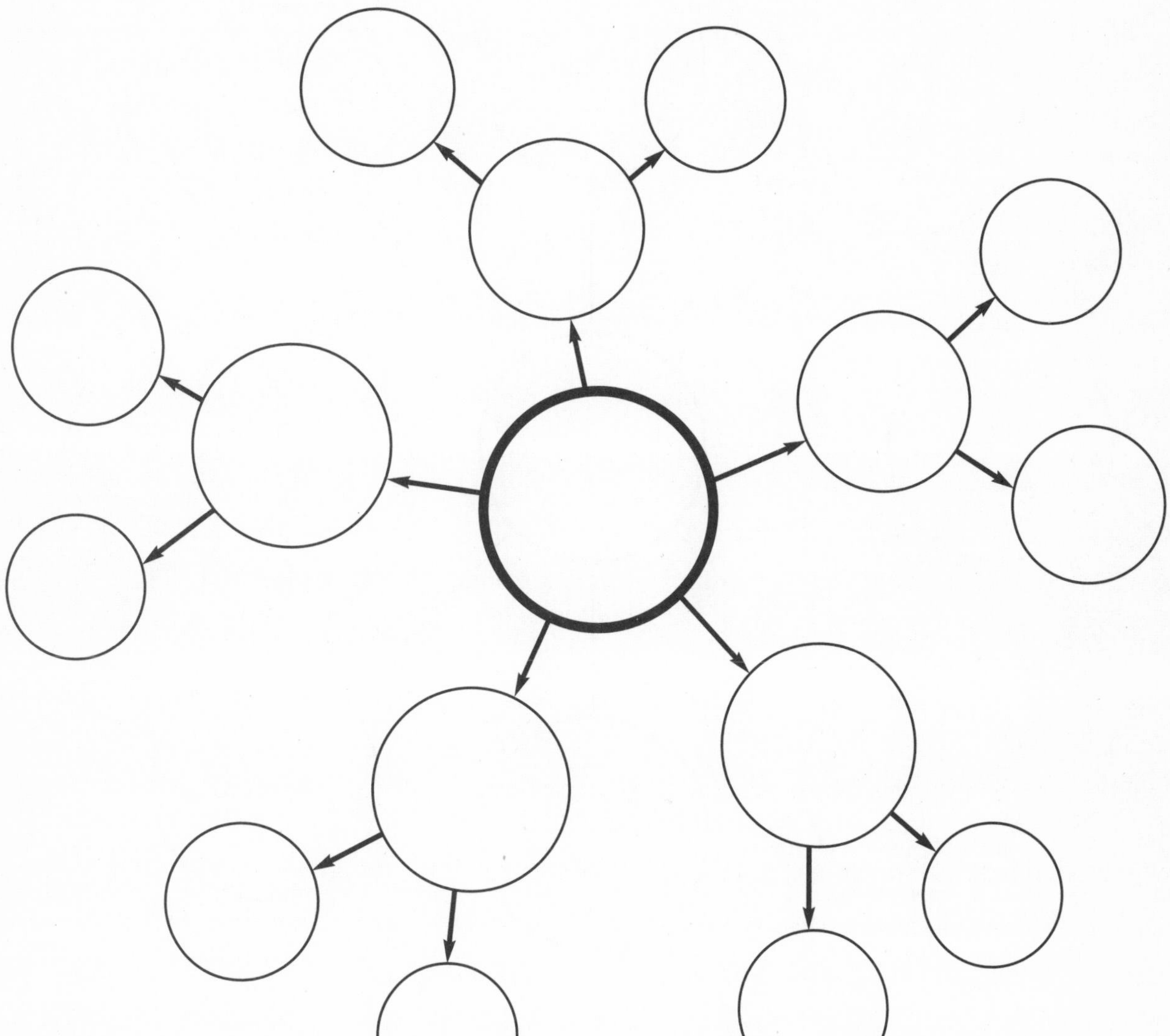

Word Web

A *word web* is a graphic planner that analyzes and gives alternatives for a specific word. Word webs are often used to list synonyms, antonyms, or rhyming words.

How it Works: A specific word is listed in the center. Alternatives for the word are written in the outer circles. There can be as many branches on a word web as needed.

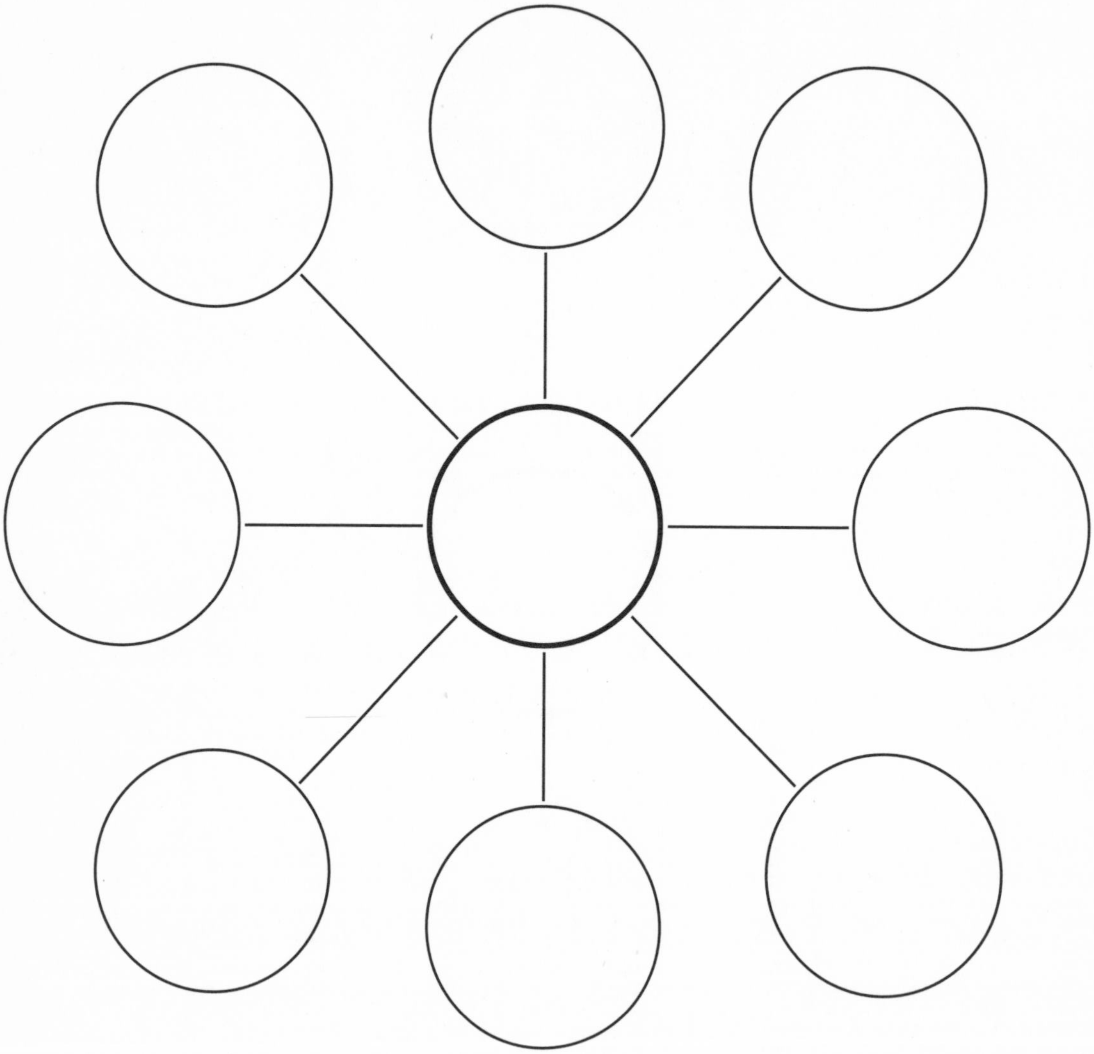

Story Map

A *story map*, sometimes called a detail chart, is a graphic planner that lists vital information to be included in a news article, report, or informative story.

How it Works: Before writing begins, all of the important details are gathered and listed in an organized fashion. Mapping is a good way of making sure important facts are included in a story. The title or headline is the first line.

by:

Opening sentence:

Who?
What?
When?
Where?
Why or how?

Conclusion:

Venn Diagram

A *Venn diagram* is a graphic planner used for comparing and contrasting two things (people, places, events, ideas, and so on).

How It Works: Similarities and differences between things are organized by placing individual characteristics in either the left or right section and common characteristics within the overlapping section.

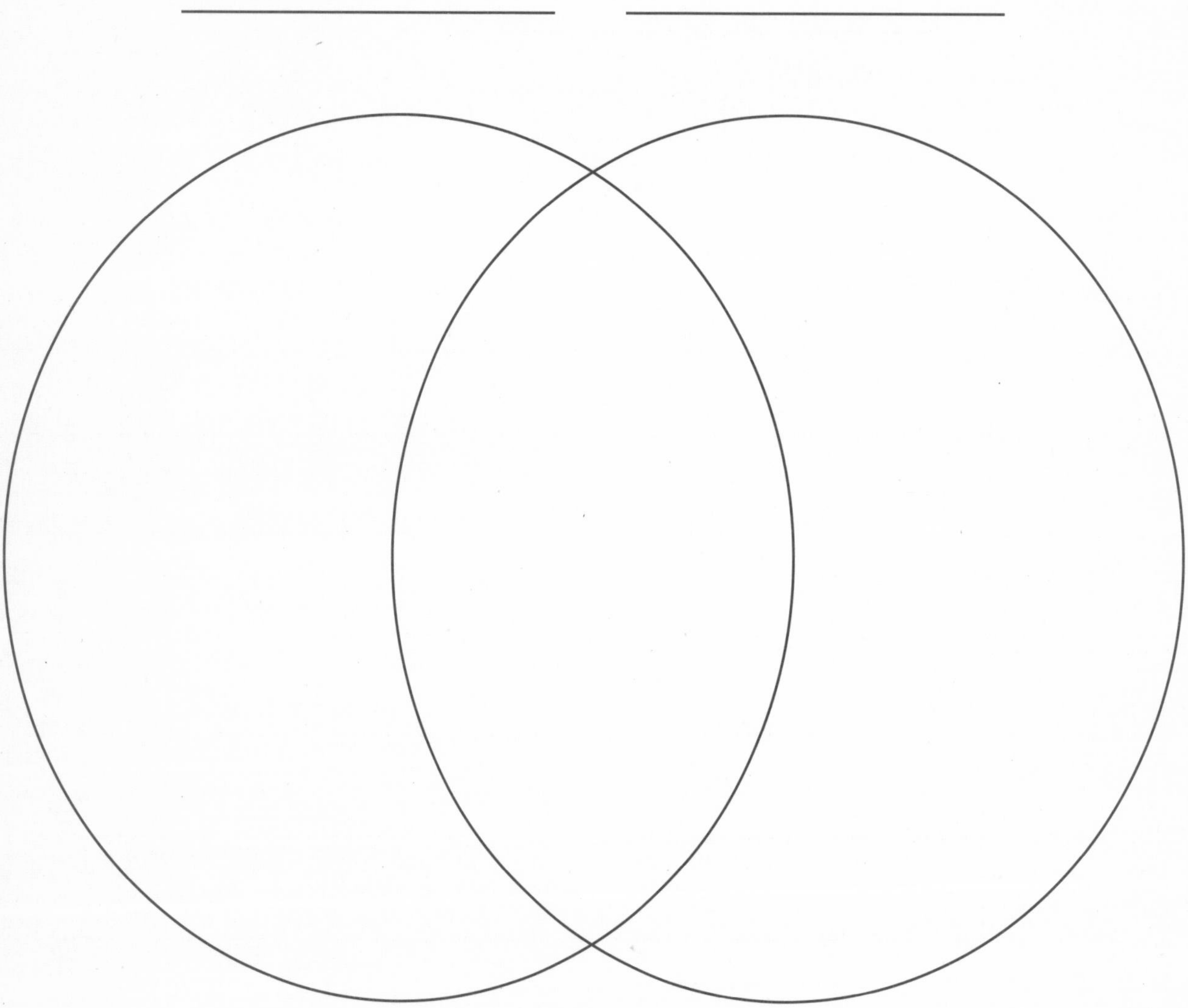

Paragraph Plan and Attribute Checklist

Paragraph Plan

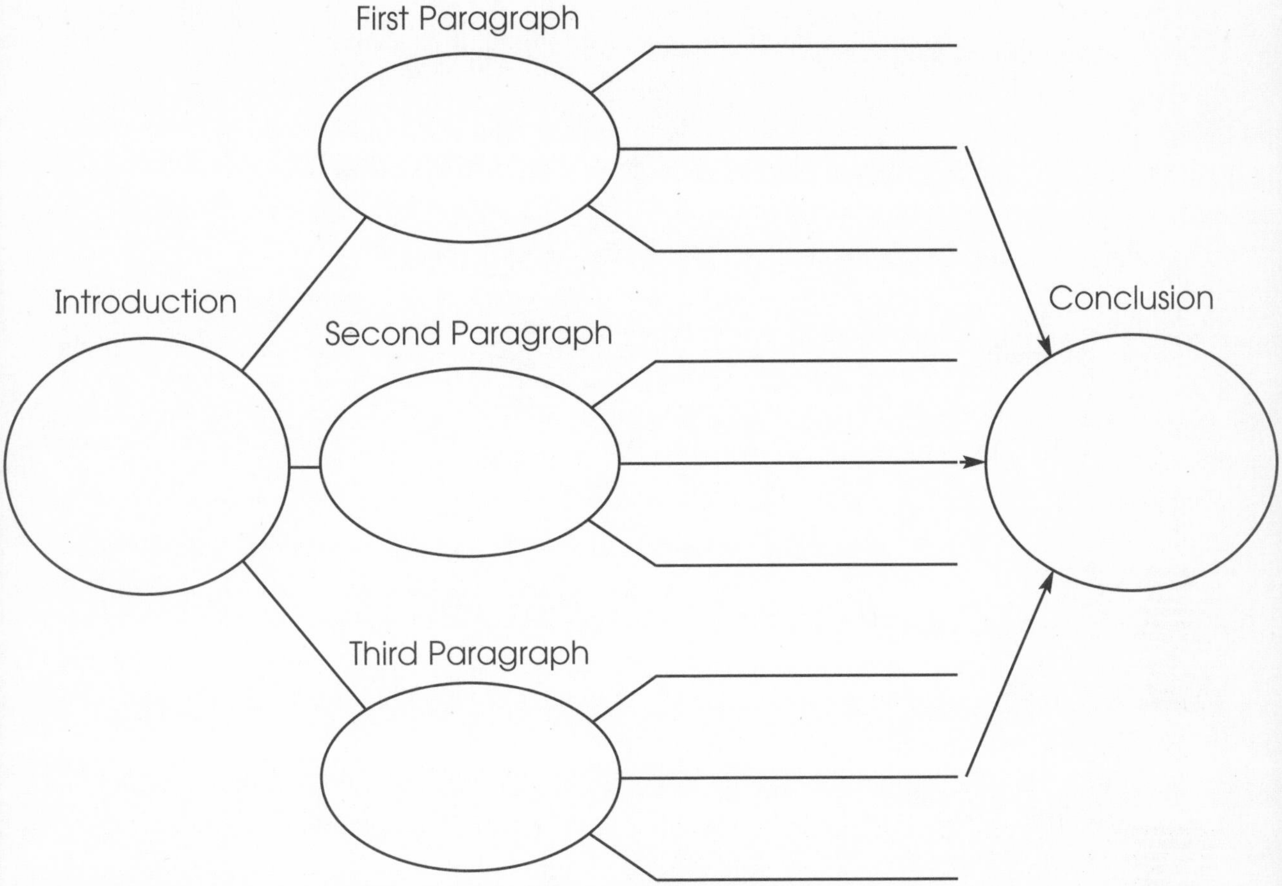

My chosen audience is:

Attribute Checklist

- ☐ This writing addresses my chosen audience:____________________
- ☐ The topic ________________ has a clear focus:________________.
- ☐ Each paragraph has a topic sentence.
- ☐ Each sentence in a paragraph supports the topic.
- ☐ Each sentence has a subject and a predicate.
- ☐ The sentences have a variety of word orders.
- ☐ I have checked for and added interesting word choices.
- ☐ I have checked capitals and punctuation.

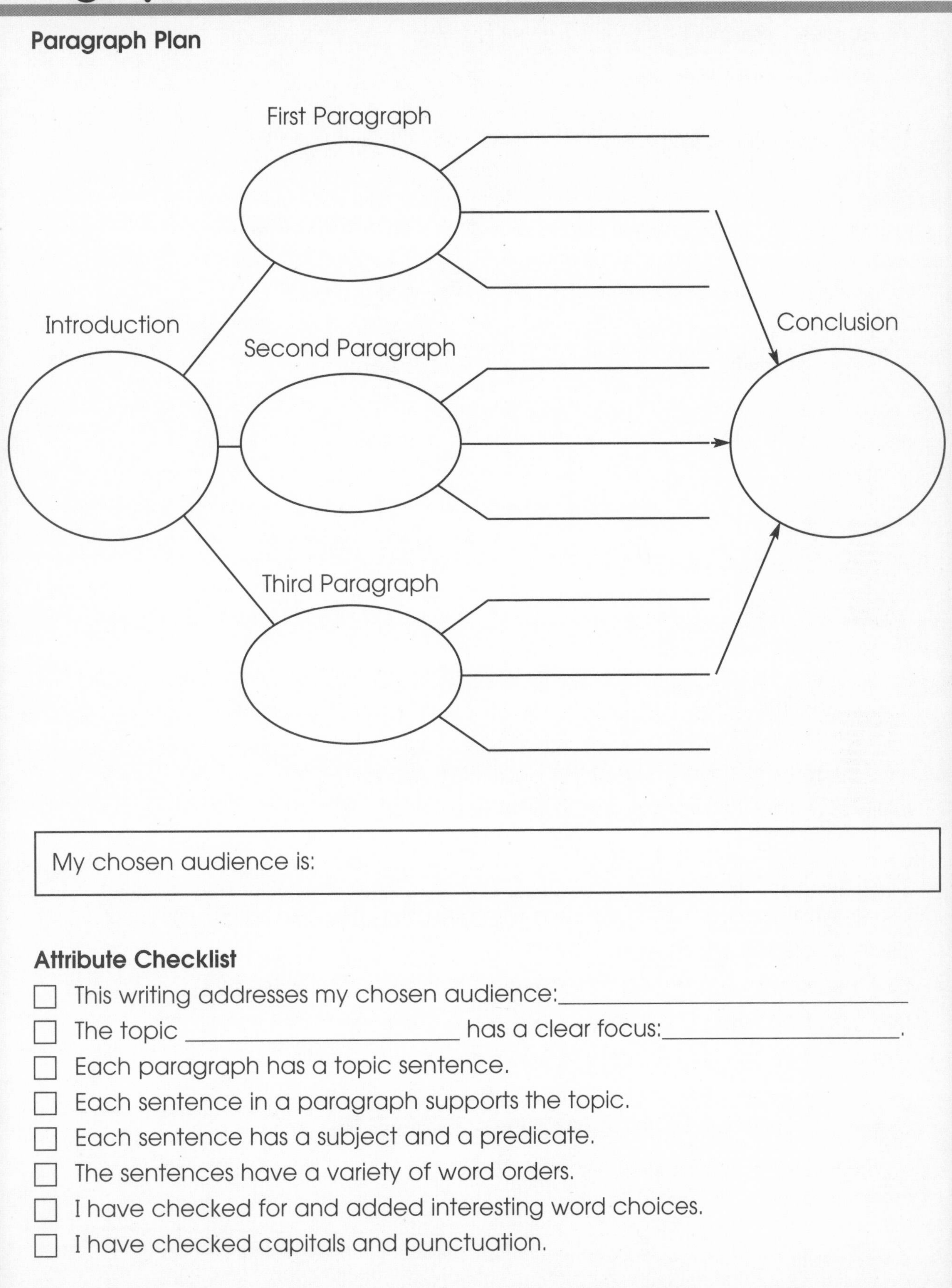

Editing Checklist

Proofreading Marks

Jen ^	Insert word	JEn (E struck)	Lowercase
^,	Add a comma	jen (triple underline)	Capitalize
"Jen"	Add quotation marks	¶	New paragraph
Jen's	Add apostrophe	... (stet)	Let it stand
~~Jen~~	Delete	(sp)	Spelling
^.	Add period		

Make sure you

Capitalize the title.

Punctuate the title.

- Titles of long works are underlined.
- Titles of short works are in quotation marks. (" ")

Capitalize the first word in each sentence.

Capitalize proper nouns. (Sue, Texas, Monday)

Indent paragraphs.

Use quotation marks and commas with direct quotes. (He said, " ")

Use complete sentences.

Use the proper punctuation mark at the ends of sentences. (. ? !)

Use apostrophes in contractions. (I'm, don't, she'll)

Use apostrophes in possessive nouns. (Tim's bike)

Use commas in a series. (cats, dogs, and mice)

Use transitional words. (then, afterwards, meanwhile)

Use descriptive words. (bumpy, tiny, quick)

Name **Week #1**

Day #1

Underline with three short lines the first letter of each word that should be capitalized in the sentence.

1. shirley made two new canadian friends in quebec city last august.

Write a contraction for each pair of words.

2. it is _____________ I am _____________

Add the correct end punctuation to the sentence.

3. Will Father and Mr. Jackson be on the same bowling team

Change the singular nouns to plural nouns.

4. candy _____________ knife _____________

Day #2

Underline with three short lines the first letter of each word that should be capitalized in the sentence.

1. the children's favorite teacher is mr. alberts.

Write a contraction for each pair of words.

2. that is _____________ we are _____________

Add the correct end punctuation to the sentence.

3. Our team won

Change the singular nouns to plural nouns.

4. piano _____________ ax _____________

Day #3

Underline with three short lines the first letter of each word that should be capitalized in the sentence.

1. we watched the parade on new year's day.

Write a contraction for each pair of words.

2. what is _____________ we have _____________

Add the correct end punctuation to the sentence.

3. Do you remember when Neil Armstrong walked on the moon

Change the singular nouns to plural nouns.

4. potato _____________ army _____________

Day #4

Underline with three short lines the first letter of each word that should be capitalized in the sentence.

1. I think professor jenkins left a stack of books on the desk.

Write a contraction for each pair of words.

2. he is _____________ you have _____________

Add the correct end punctuation to the sentence.

3. Having chicken pox can be very annoying

Change the singular nouns to plural nouns.

4. copy _____________ tooth _____________

Assessment #1

Underline with three short lines the first letter of each word that should be capitalized in the sentences and add correct end punctuation.

1. jackie and i took a train to new york on may 18, 1990

2. did dr. swift give you a penicillin shot

3. my uncle's friend, judge w. heinz, is german

4. did you see pepper chase that brown cat up the tree

5. how exciting

Write a contraction for each pair of words.

6. you have ______________ we have ______________

7. it is ______________ that is ______________

Change the singular nouns to plural nouns.

8. candy ______________ army ______________

9. piano ______________ potato ______________

10. tooth ______________ knife ______________

Name **Week #2**

prewrite/brainstorm

Descriptive writing is interesting and effective. Think of your favorite fruit or vegetable. Use adjectives to describe it in the word web below.

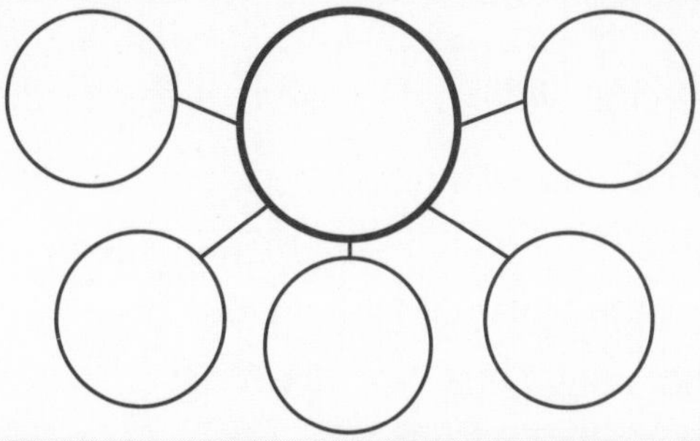

Day #1

draft

When you look at your web describing your favorite fruit or vegetable, you will want to focus on one main idea. Write a paragraph using as many adjectives from your web as you can.

____

____

____

____

Day #2

revise

Look at your paragraph about your favorite fruit or vegetable. Do all of the sentences talk about the same idea? What information could you add? What sentences would you change? Write out your changes.

____

____

____

____

Day #3

proofread

Look at your final paragraph about your favorite fruit or vegetable. Are all of the words spelled correctly? Did you capitalize words that need to be capitalized? Proofread your paragraph.

- ❐ ✓ Capitalization Mistakes
- ❐ ✓ Odd Grammar
- ❐ ✓ Punctuation Mistakes
- ❐ ✓ Spelling Mistakes

Day #4

Name

Assessment

Assessment #2

publish

Now it is time to publish your writing. Write your final copy on the lines below.

MAKE SURE it turns out:

- NEAT—Make sure there are no wrinkles, creases, or holes.
- CLEAN—Erase any smudges or dirty spots.
- EASY TO READ—Use your best handwriting and good spacing between words.

Name

Week # 3

Day #1

Underline with three short lines the first letter of each word that should be capitalized in the sentence.

1. Tony started at his new school on september 3.

Write a contraction for each pair of words.

2. had not ______________ there is ______________

Add the correct punctuation to the sentence.

3. Barbara Bertha and Betty live on Fern Ave near Dr Jones

Change the singular nouns to plural nouns.

4. calf ______________ shelf ______________

Day #2

Underline with three short lines the first letter of each word that should be capitalized in the sentence.

1. is west virginia a separate state?

Write a contraction for each pair of words.

2. they will ______________ where is ______________

Add the correct punctuation to the sentence.

3. Yes I did go camping on August 10 1998

Change the singular nouns to plural nouns.

4. duty ______________ grocery ______________

Day #3

Underline with three short lines the first letter of each word that should be capitalized in the sentence.

1. "ode to autumn" is uncle joe's favorite poem.

Write a contraction for each pair of words.

2. should not ______________ we will ______________

Add the correct punctuation to the sentence.

3. That batters bat broke into two pieces

Change the singular nouns to plural nouns.

4. enemy ______________ city ______________

Day #4

Underline with three short lines the first letter of each word that should be capitalized in the sentence.

1. bobby crossed to the south side of fountain road.

Write a contraction for each pair of words.

2. were not ______________ are not ______________

Add the correct punctuation to the sentence.

3. B.J. hasnt finished her homework yet

Change the singular nouns to plural nouns.

4. cupful ______________ loaf ______________

Name Week # 3

Assessment # 3

Assessment

Using proofreading marks, underline with three short lines the first letter of each word that should be capitalized in the sentences and add the correct punctuation.

1. donnas dog, skipper, ran across meyer ave to palm park

2. have you seen mother and aunt Vivienne

3. look out

4. my parents and i visited dr bensons office on march 2 1999

5. gail jerry and i walked to the beach

Write a contraction for each pair of words.

6. we will ______________ they will ______________

7. have not ______________ were not ______________

8. where is ______________ there is ______________

Change the singular nouns to plural nouns.

9. calf ______________ loaf ______________

10. grocery ______________ city ______________

Name **Week # 4**

prewrite/brainstorm — Day #1

To begin writing a multi-paragraph essay, you first must decide on a topic. From the list below, pick a topic that you would like to write about. On a separate sheet of paper, draw the clustering map. Write your topic in the middle circle. Now, brainstorm and add as many branches as you wish.

- a favorite vacation spot
- why you like a special friend
- a friend who is very intelligent
- why you like skating
- your favorite holiday
- the funniest person you know

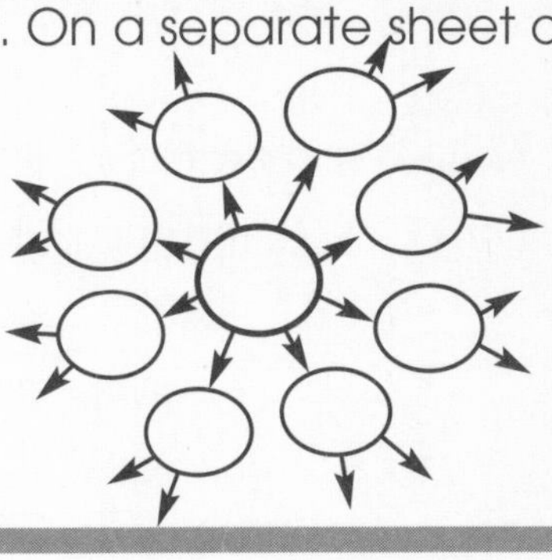

draft — Day #2

Practice writing an introduction paragraph. Write an introduction paragraph about the topic you picked from the list. Use the ideas you created when you brainstormed to help you to write an introduction paragraph.

revise — Day #3

Read what you wrote yesterday. Can you be more specific? Do you need to put your sentences in a different order? Rewrite your ideas in a new paragraph. Be sure your ideas are complete sentences. Change nouns, verbs, and adjectives to more specific words.

proofread — Day #4

Proofread your new paragraph. Are any words misspelled? Did you use the correct verb form? Make sure your capitalization and punctuation are correct. Mark the corrections with proofreading marks.

- ❒ ✓ Capitalization Mistakes
- ❒ ✓ Odd Grammar
- ❒ ✓ Punctuation Mistakes
- ❒ ✓ Spelling Mistakes

0-7682-3225-2 *Write 4 Today*

Assessment

Assessment # 4

publish

Now it is time to publish your writing. Write your final copy on the lines below.

MAKE SURE it turns out:

- NEAT—Make sure there are no wrinkles, creases, or holes.
- CLEAN—Erase any smudges or dirty spots.
- EASY TO READ—Use your best handwriting and good spacing between words.

Name **Week # 5**

Day #1

Underline with three short lines the first letter of each word that should be capitalized.

1. on december 7, 1941, the japanese attacked pearl harbor.

Read the sentences. Choose the sentence in which the subject and verb agree.

2. a. The daffodils is all blooming on the hillside.
   b. A gentle rain wash the drowsiness from the waking earth.
   c. Seedlings wake from their long sleep.

Use proofreading marks to correct the punctuation.

3. After all of that we still didn't know how Eduardo would get to Johns game

Choose the correct spelling.

4. a. brot b. broght c. brought d. brougth

Day #2

Underline with three short lines the first letter of each word that should be capitalized.

1. our old house was in central city, kansas.

Read the sentences. Choose the sentence in which the subject and verb agree.

2. a. My mother worries that her garden will not grow.
   b. Dad say that this autumn we should have a good harvest.
   c. Along the riverbank, my brothers hunts for frogs.

Use proofreading marks to correct the punctuation.

3. Cinderella do you want to go to the ball now asked her fairy godmother

Choose the correct spelling.

4. a. because b. becuz c. becaus d. becuse

Day #3

Underline with three short lines the first letter of each word that should be capitalized.

1. "could we please," carl asked mr. chen, "have some ice cream?"

Read the sentences. Choose the sentence in which the subject and verb agree.

2. a. The plow and the oxen stands ready to plant another crop.
   b. Our coop is full of squawking chickens and crowing roosters.
   c. In the pigpen, hogs searches for their morning food.

Use proofreading marks to correct the punctuation.

3. Our teacher moved here from Bangor Maine on August 4 2002

Choose the correct spelling.

4. Kyle _______ want to play. a. didnt b. did'nt c. didnt' d. didn't

Day #4

Underline with three short lines the first letter of each word that should be capitalized.

1. dr. shard said, "come by my office on tuesday."

Read the sentences. Choose the sentence in which the subject and verb agree.

2. a. Before the winter came, we harvested our crops.
   b. We'll plants beans next year.
   c. Our crops fills four wagons.

Use proofreading marks to correct the punctuation.

3. Mayor Hill said Please, think about it

Choose the correct spelling.

4. Shantal loves to go to the library with her _______. a. familie b. falmily c. familee d. family

Asse sment # 5

Certai vords or phrases must be capitalized. Choose the sentence that shows the corre t capitalization.

1. a. rs. Small moved here from san francisco, California.
   b. was written by a very talented author named lois lowry.
   c. ıd said, "that book is fascinating."
   d. om gave me a copy of the book for my birthday on May 1.

2. a. T e geese remind me of life in Canada.
   b. L asked Hope, "will you go to Texas for vacation?"
   c. O neighbor, mr. Kaminski, is very kind.
   d. W en I grow up, I want to write a book like the harry potter books.

Read eac sentence. Circle the form of the verb that agrees with the subject.

3. In the orning, we (has, have) to feed the horses, chickens, and hogs.
4. Dad (l ve, leaves) after breakfast and (work, works) in the fields all day.
5. All of th household chores (are, is) finished by noon.

Use proofre ding marks to correct the punctuation.

6. Shanti c ed Ahmal and said can you travel with me and my family"

7. Charlene ant you find the golden necklace you bought in Dallas Texas

Choose the s tence with no spelling mistakes.

8. a. The po d rippled becuz of the breeze.
   b. We bro ht our brand new fishing poles with us.
   c. The wo s we brougth made excellent bait!
   d. We ba d our hooks and brought our lines over to the pond.

9. a. It didnt ke long before my brother felt a tug.
   b. He slow rot the line in, pulling aginst the fish.
   c. Because e fish was strong, it made him work hard!
   d. A few ra ow trout would make a great dinner for our falmily!

10. a. Mom sho ed us how to clean fish so she didnt' have to do it alone.
    b. Dad didn mind teaching us the right way to cook them.
    c. The whol amilie sat down to a delicious meal.
    d. Today wa y favorite familee fishing day ever!

Name

Week # 6

prewrite/brainstorm

In week #4 you wrote the topic paragraph of an essay. To continue writing your multi-paragraph essay, you must decide what you want to write in your supporting paragraph. On a separate sheet of paper, draw a clustering map. Write your topic (week #4) in the middle circle. Now, brainstorm and add as many branches as you wish.

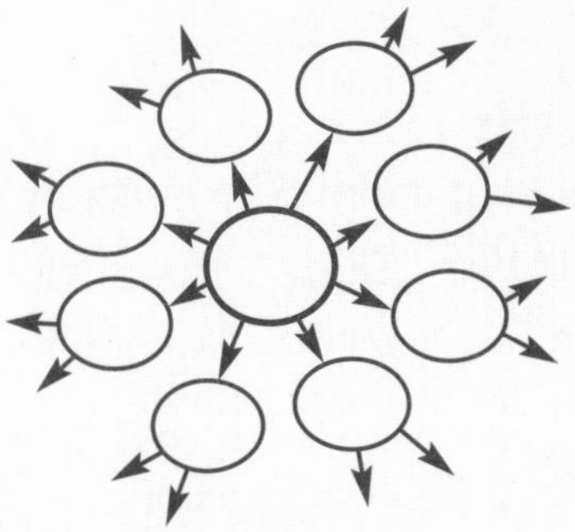

Day #1

draft

Now draft the supporting paragraph. Write about one idea that supports your topic. Use the ideas you created when you brainstormed to help you.

____

____

____

____

Day #2

revise

Read what you wrote yesterday. Can you be more specific? Do you need to put your sentences in a different order? Rewrite your ideas in a new paragraph. Be sure your ideas are complete sentences. Change nouns, verbs, and adjectives to more specific words.

____

____

____

____

Day #3

proofread

Proofread your new paragraph. Are any words misspelled? Did you use the correct verb form? Make sure your capitalization and punctuation are correct. Mark the corrections with proofreading marks.

- ❐ ✓ Capitalization Mistakes
- ❐ ✓ Odd Grammar
- ❐ ✓ Punctuation Mistakes
- ❐ ✓ Spelling Mistakes

Day #4

Name Week #

Assessment # 6

Assessment

publish

Now it is time to publish your writing. Write your final copy on the lines below.

MAKE SURE it turns out:

- NEAT—Make sure there are no wrinkles, creases, or holes.
- CLEAN—Erase any smudges or dirty spots.
- EASY TO READ—Use your best handwriting and good spacing between words.

Name

Week #7

Day #1

Underline with three short lines the first letter of words that need to be capitalized.

1. when i think of kentucky, i think of the kentucky derby.

Underline the complete subject and circle the simple subject in the sentence.

2. The best horse race in the world has many beautiful horses.

Use proofreading marks to correct the punctuation in the sentence.

3. When you think of Kentucky what do you think of

Circle the correct word in the sentence.

4. The (principle/principal) of my school visited Kentucky.

Day #2

Underline with three short lines the first letter of words that need to be capitalized.

1. when i think of indiana, i think of the indy 500.

Underline the complete subject and circle the simple subject in the sentence.

2. That famous car race is my dad's favorite sporting event.

Use proofreading marks to correct the punctuation in the sentence.

3. Massachusetts reminds me of the Boston Marathon the Boston Red Sox and the Boston Tea Party

Circle the correct word in the sentence.

4. Do you want to go (there/their/they're)?

Day #3

Underline with three short lines the first letter of words that need to be capitalized.

1. i think of the dallas cowboys and the houston astros when i think of texas.

Underline the complete subject and circle the simple subject in the sentence.

2. The football players in Texas are strong.

Use proofreading marks to correct the punctuation in the sentence.

3. Some states have several sports teams, like football baseball and basketball

Circle the correct word in the sentence.

4. I think football is (grate/great)!

Day #4

Underline with three short lines the first letter of words that need to be capitalized.

1. rhode island and south dakota don't have professional football teams.

Underline the complete subject and circle the simple subject in the sentence.

2. Sports provide entertainment for millions of people.

Use proofreading marks to correct the punctuation in the sentence.

3. Millions of people watch competitions on television listen to the games on the radio or go to the games

Circle the correct word in the sentence.

4. Do you have a favorite sports (team/teem)?

Name Week #

Assessment #7

Assessment

Read the paragraph. Find the eight errors in the paragraph and correct them using proofreading marks.

Excited crowds in many states attend sporting events every week. Fans follow

there favorite teems What is your favorite sport I like a lot of sports. I like to watch

the Yankees the red Sox and the blue Jays when they play.

Now rewrite the paragraph correctly. In the first sentence, underline the complete subject and circle the simple subject.

Name **Week # 8**

prewrite/brainstorm

To finish the multi-paragraph essay you worked on in week #4 and week #6, you must decide what to write in your conclusion paragraph. On a separate sheet of paper, draw a clustering map. Write your topic in the center circle. Then write your main ideas in other circles.

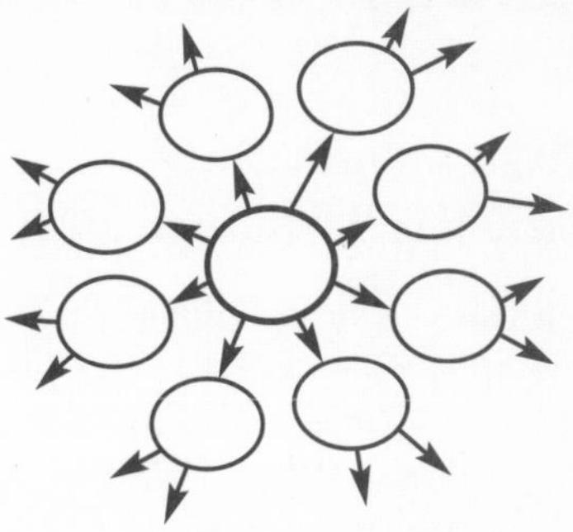

Day #1

draft

Use the ideas you brainstormed to draft your conclusion paragraph. Write a paragraph that sums up your topic.

____

____

____

____

____

Day #2

revise

Read what you wrote yesterday. Can you be more specific? Do you need to put your sentences in a different order? Rewrite your ideas in a new paragraph. Be sure your ideas are complete sentences. Change nouns, verbs, and adjectives to more specific words.

____

____

____

____

Day #3

proofread

Proofread your new paragraph. Are any words misspelled? Did you use the correct verb form? Make sure your capitalization and punctuation are correct. Mark the corrections with proofreading marks.

- ❒ ✓ Capitalization Mistakes
- ❒ ✓ Odd Grammar
- ❒ ✓ Punctuation Mistakes
- ❒ ✓ Spelling Mistakes

Day #4

Name

Assessment

Assessment # 8

publish

Now it is time to publish your writing. Write your final copy on the lines below.

MAKE SURE it turns out:

- NEAT—Make sure there are no wrinkles, creases, or holes.
- CLEAN—Erase any smudges or dirty spots.
- EASY TO READ—Use your best handwriting and good spacing between words.

Name **Week # 9**

Use proofreading marks to correct the capitalization errors in the sentence.

1. the First african american to play major league Baseball was jackie robinson.

Underline the verbs in the sentences.

2. Divers see underwater with a face mask. The face mask also keeps out the water.

Put the quotation marks and the punctuation marks in the correct places in the sentence.

3. The teacher said Some areas of the Sahara Desert get less than one inch of rain a year!

Circle the correct word to complete the sentence.

4. The streetlight (shown/shone) brightly.

Day #1

Use proofreading marks to correct the capitalization errors in the sentence.

1. Tiger woods was the first golfer of african-american Ancestry to win the masters Tournament.

Underline the verbs in the sentences.

2. Divers strap air tanks to their backs. A tank holds compressed air for the diver to breathe.

Put the quotation marks and the punctuation marks in the correct places in the sentence.

3. Do plants grow in the desert asked Beth.

Circle the correct word to complete the sentence.

4. The letter began, "(Dear/Deer) Mr. President."

Day #2

Use proofreading marks to correct the capitalization errors in the sentence.

1. Muhammad ali was an american boxing Champion.

Underline the verbs in the sentences.

2. An air hose moves air from the tank to a scuba diver's mouth. The diver releases exhaled air into the water.

Put the quotation marks and the punctuation marks in the correct places in the sentence.

3. Plants grow quickly said Shannon. They complete their life cycle in about six weeks.

Circle the correct word to complete the sentence.

4. (Whose/Who's) backpack is this?

Use proofreading marks to correct the capitalization errors in the sentence.

1. Many other african americans have won Medals in the olympic games.

Underline the verbs in the sentences.

2. Divers swim easily with fins. A wet suit protects the diver's body.

Put the quotation marks and the punctuation marks in the correct places in the sentence.

3. Anthony asked How do plants get water in the desert

Circle the correct word to complete the sentence.

4. During our game, the baseball soared (threw/through) Mr. Nantucket's window.

Name

Assessment

Assessment # 9

Use proofreading marks to correct the capitalization errors in the sentences.

1. American track star carl lewis won nine Gold Medals in the olympic games.
2. Jackie joyner-kersee was the first woman to Win consecutive heptathlon competitions in the olympics.
3. Michael jordan was one of the best and most exciting Players in the national basketball association.

Underline the verbs in the sentences.

4. Divers near the water's surface breathe through a snorkel tube.
5. A weight belt holds a diver down in the water.

Put the quotation marks and the punctuation marks in the correct places in the sentence.

6. Some desert plants have long roots that go deep into the soil said Rosa.
7. Carmello said Desert animals can go for a long time without water

Circle the correct word to complete the sentence.

8. Start your pen pal letter with, "(Deer/Dear) Pen Pal."
9. (Who's/Whose) house should we study at?
10. The game was tied after Joe (threw/through) the ball to Sara.

Name **Week #10**

prewrite/brainstorm

Narrative writing tells a story. Use a story map to plan a story about a new student beginning fifth grade.

1. a. setting: ____________________
   b. characters: ____________________
   c. problem: ____________________
2. first event: ____________________
3. second event: ____________________
4. third event: ____________________
5. resolution: ____________________

Day #1

draft

Begin your narrative by writing an introduction paragraph. Set the stage for your story by describing the characters, setting, and first event. Include the problem and an interesting opening sentence that will make your reader want to keep reading.

____
____
____
____

Day #2

revise

Now it's time to revise your paragraph. Read your first draft. Can you be more specific? Do you have information that you do not need? Do you want to change your sentence order? Rewrite your ideas in a new paragraph. Change nouns, verbs, and adjectives to more specific words and use complete sentences.

____
____
____

Day #3

proofread

Proofread your new paragraph. Are any words misspelled? Did you use the correct verb form? Make sure your capitalization and punctuation are correct. Mark the corrections with proofreading marks.

- ❐ ✓ Capitalization Mistakes
- ❐ ✓ Odd Grammar
- ❐ ✓ Punctuation Mistakes
- ❐ ✓ Spelling Mistakes

Day #4

Name

Week # 10

Assessment

Assessment # 10

publish

Now it is time to publish your writing. Write your final copy on the lines below.

MAKE SURE it turns out:

- NEAT—Make sure there are no wrinkles, creases, or holes.
- CLEAN—Erase any smudges or dirty spots.
- EASY TO READ—Use your best handwriting and good spacing between words.

Name

Week # 11

Day #1

Circle the choice that shows the right capitalization.

1. a. *Harry Potter And The Order Of The Phoenix*
   b. *Harry Potter and the Order of the Phoenix*
   c. *Harry Potter and The Order of The Phoenix*

Circle the choice that shows the right spelling.

2. ________ is wrong here.
   a. Sumthing
   b. Some thing
   c. Something
   d. Sum Thing

Read the pair of sentences. Rewrite the pair correctly.

3. She don't get it. Yes, she do! ____________________

Commas separate words in a series of three or more. Colons introduce a list. Using proofreading marks, add the missing punctuation to the sentence.

4. Pack these things in a backpack for the bus trip a snack a water bottle sunscreen and a hat.

Day #2

Circle the choice that shows the right capitalization.

1. a. *My Dog is from Pluto*
   b. *My dog Is from pluto*
   c. *My Dog Is from Pluto*

Circle the choice that shows the right spelling.

2. My ________ music is jazz.
   a. favrite
   b. faverite
   c. favarite
   d. favorite

Read the pair of sentences. Rewrite the pair correctly.

3. He don't like it. Yes, he do! ____________________

Commas separate words in a series of three or more. Colons introduce a list. Using proofreading marks, add the missing punctuation to the sentence.

4. Do not bring these items to Camp Porcupine gum candy money and electronic gadgets.

Day #3

Circle the choice that shows the right capitalization.

1. a. *Tuck Everlasting*
   b. *Tuck EverLasting*
   c. *Tuck everlasting*

Circle the choice that shows the right spelling.

2. We ______ finished the test.
   a. finely
   b. finelly
   c. finally
   d. finaly

Read the pair of sentences. Rewrite the pair correctly.

3. It don't matter. Yes, it do! ____________________

Commas separate words in a series of three or more. Colons introduce a list. Using proofreading marks, add the missing punctuation to the sentence.

4. Campers counselors and activity leaders are assigned to units at Camp Porcupine.

Day #4

Circle the choice that shows the right capitalization.

1. a. *Harriet The Spy*
   b. *Harriet the Spy*
   c. *Harriet The spy*

Circle the choice that shows the right spelling.

2. ________ house is white with a blue roof.
   a. Or
   b. Hour
   c. Oure
   d. Our

Read the pair of sentences. Rewrite the pair correctly.

2. My mom don't want me to learn this. Yes, she do! ____________________

Commas separate words in a series of three or more. Colons introduce a list. Using proofreading marks, add the missing punctuation to the sentence.

3. Each unit has these structures six camper tents two staff tents two bathrooms and one shower house.

Name Week #

Assessment #11

Assessment

Circle the choice that shows the right capitalization.

1. a. *Island of The Blue Dolphins*
   b. *Island Of The Blue Dolphins*
   c. *Island of the Blue Dolphins*

2. a. *The Westing game*
   b. *The Westing Game*
   c. *the Westing Game*

Read the pairs of sentences. Rewrite each pair correctly.

3. My dad don't notice if I speak incorrectly. Yes, he do!

____

____

4. My family don't care about school. Yes, it do!

____

____

Commas separate words in a series of three or more. Colons introduce a list. Usir proofreading marks, add the missing punctuation to the sentence.

5. Eagle Coyote and Grizzly Bear are the three girls' units.
6. The boys' units are Fox Hawk and Elk.
7. You must do these lodge chores when your unit has meal duty set the table serve food clear the dishes clean the tables and sweep the floors.

Rewrite these words correctly on the lines.

8. sumthing ______________________________
9. faverit ______________________________
10. finaly ______________________________

Name

Week #12

prewrite/brainstorm

Continue writing the narrative you started on week 10. Look back at the first two events on your story map. Make a list of descriptive words about the second event.

second event:

Day #1

draft

Now draft a paragraph describing the second event that happened when a new student began fifth grade. Use the ideas you wrote on your brainstorming list.

Day #2

revise

Now it's time to revise your paragraphs about the new student. Read your first draft. Can you be more specific? Do you have information that you do not need? Do you want to change your sentence order? Rewrite your paragraph. Change nouns, verbs, and adjectives to more specific words and use complete sentences.

Day #3

proofread

Proofread your paragraph about the new student. Are any words misspelled? Did you use the correct verb form? Make sure your capitalization and punctuation are correct. Mark the corrections with proofreading marks.

- ❒ ✓ Capitalization Mistakes
- ❒ ✓ Odd Grammar
- ❒ ✓ Punctuation Mistakes
- ❒ ✓ Spelling Mistakes

Day #4

Assessment

Assess nent #12

publish

Now it is ne to publish your writing. Write your final copy on the lines below.

MAKE SU it turns out:

- NE —Make sure there are no wrinkles, creases, or holes.
- CL N—Erase any smudges or dirty spots.
- EA TO READ—Use your best handwriting and good spacing between words.

Day #1

Underline with three short lines the first letter of words that need to be capitalized.

1. did the movie *around the world in 80 days* win an academy award in 1956?

Draw a line under the complete predicate. Circle the predicate verb.

2. Joan and I cheered for our favorite team.

Add quotation marks, underlining, and punctuation where necessary in the sentence.

3. The Olympic Games were held in Stockholm Sweden in 1912 replied vivian

Homonyms are words that sound alike but have different meanings and spellings. Circle the correct words in the sentence.

4. My library book was (dew/due) last (week/weak).

Day #2

Underline with three short lines the first letter of words that need to be capitalized.

1. robert burns, the poet, wrote "auld lang syne."

Draw a line under the complete predicate. Circle the predicate verb.

2. Chris dropped one more quarter into the machine.

Add quotation marks, underlining, and punctuation where necessary in the sentence.

3. Monica yelled Wow did you see that car

Circle the correct words in the sentence.

4. Did those (ate/eight) (flowers/flours) come from your yard?

Day #3

Underline with three short lines the first letter of words that need to be capitalized.

1. does grandpa get the *chicago sun times* or the *chicago tribune*?

Draw a line under the complete predicate. Circle the predicate verb.

2. The clerk examined the jacket carefully.

Add quotation marks, underlining, and punctuation where necessary in the sentence.

3. Look out screamed Andy

Circle the correct words in the sentence.

4. Frances (scent/sent) her (aunt/ant) a birthday card.

Day #4

Underline with three short lines the first letter of words that need to be capitalized.

1. we're going to an italian restaurant on friday night after we read *strega nona*.

Draw a line under the complete predicate. Circle the predicate verb.

2. Margie's dog, Bandit, is a frisky animal.

Add quotation marks, underlining, and punctuation where necessary in the sentence.

3. Bobby our class president took charge of today's meeting

Circle the correct words in the sentence.

4. (Too/To/Two) dollars is a (fare/fair) price.

Name **Week # 13**

Assessment # 13

Assessment

Using proofreading marks, mark the first letter of words that need to be capitalized and add punctuation to the sentences.

1. i received the book *the life cycle book of cats* from grandmother

2. will judge j.t. otis preside today

3. dad, *the los angeles times* was not delivered this morning said doug

4. dorians deli carries turkish candy remarked peggy

Draw a line under the complete predicate in the sentences. Circle the predicate verb.

5. My teacher asked for volunteers.

6. The birds ate all the seeds.

7. Rex and I are in the same race.

Circle the correct words in the sentences.

8. Dad (sent/scent) Mom (flower/flours) for her birthday.

9. We have (too/two) more (weeks/weaks) until this is (due/dew).

10. Can you imagine having (eight/ate) uncles and (ants/aunts)?

Name

Week #14

prewrite/brainstorm

It is time to write about the third event in the narrative you worked on in weeks 10 and 12. Look back at what you wrote for that event on your story map. Take that idea and make a list of descriptive words about the third event.

third event:

Day #1

draft

Conclude your narrative by drafting a paragraph that wraps up everything that happened when a new student began fifth grade. Use the ideas you wrote on your brainstorming list. Be sure to include the resolution to the story problem.

Day #2

revise

Now it's time to revise your paragraphs about the new student. Read your first draft. Can you be more specific? Do you have information that you do not need? Do you want to change your sentence order? Rewrite your paragraph. Change nouns, verbs, and adjectives to more specific words and use complete sentences.

Day #3

proofread

Proofread your paragraph about the new student. Are any words misspelled? Did you use the correct verb form? Make sure your capitalization and punctuation are correct. Mark the corrections with proofreading marks.

- ❒ ✓ Capitalization Mistakes
- ❒ ✓ Odd Grammar
- ❒ ✓ Punctuation Mistakes
- ❒ ✓ Spelling Mistakes

Day #4

Name

Assessment #14

Assessment

publish

Now it is time to publish your writing. Write your final copy on the lines below.

MAKE SURE it turns out:

- NEAT—Make sure there are no wrinkles, creases, or holes.
- CLEAN—Erase any smudges or dirty spots.
- EASY TO READ—Use your best handwriting and good spacing between words.

Name

Week #15

Day #1

Use proofreading marks to correct the capitalization errors in the sentence.

1. Last Winter, the students voted to have Music played in the Cafeteria during lunch on fridays.

Fill in the circle next to the correct interrogative pronoun.

2. _________ should I call in case of an emergency?
   ❍ Who ❍ Whom

Complete the sentence so it contains a direct quotation. Add quotation marks, commas, and end punctuation.

3. Ellen shouted ____

Use proofreading marks to correct the words that are not spelled correctly.

4. Have you ever wanted to shair a secret with someone without anyone else nowing?

Day #2

Use proofreading marks to correct the capitalization errors in the sentence.

1. soon after the students voted, the question was asked, "what kind of Music do students want?"

Fill in the circle next to the correct interrogative pronoun.

2. _________ left the dirty dishes in the sink?
   ❍ Who ❍ Whom

Complete the sentence so it contains a direct quotation. Add quotation marks, commas, and end punctuation.

3. Jackie said ____

Use proofreading marks to correct the words that are not spelled correctly.

4. Hears a way you can write a secret mesage. It's easey and fun to do!

Day #3

Use proofreading marks to correct the capitalization errors in the sentence.

1. The Principal let Students put classical, Oldies, Country, and rock on the ballot.

Fill in the circle next to the correct interrogative pronoun.

2. _________ called?
   ❍ Who ❍ Whom

Complete the sentence so it contains a direct quotation. Add quotation marks, commas, and end punctuation.

3. The children shouted ____

Use proofreading marks to correct the words that are not spelled correctly.

4. You shuld start bye squeezing the jooce from a lemon into a small bole.

Day

Use proofreading marks to correct the capitalization errors in the sentence.

1. Principal pecoraro said she would respect the Students' choice.

Fill in the circle next to the correct interrogative pronoun.

2. _________ do you think we should invite to the party?
   ❍ Who ❍ Whom

Complete the sentence so it contains a direct quotation. Add quotation marks, commas, and end punctuation.

3. The teacher asked ____

Use proofreading marks to correct the words that are not spelled correctly.

4. Use a toothpick two write your secret message with lemon jooce. Let it drie.

Assessment #15

Assessment

Use proofreading marks to correct the capitalization errors in the sentences.

1. Principal pecoraro said that she had her own Music likes and dislikes.
2. The Students voted to let the teachers and the Principal vote, too.
3. you can hear the results of the Vote every friday at lunch!

Fill in the circle next to the correct interrogative pronoun.

4. _____ took my sunglasses?

   ❍ Who ❍ Whom

5. _____ is responsible for this mess?

   ❍ Who ❍ Whom

6. To _____ did you give the prize?

   ❍ who ❍ whom

Complete the sentence so it contains a direct quotation. Add quotation marks, commas, and end punctuation.

7. Patty exclaimed ____
8. "Will you," Linda asked ______________________________________

Use proofreading marks to correct the words that are not spelled correctly.

9. Ask an adult too put the paper in an oven. The oven shuld be heated to 350 degrees for eight to ten minutes.

10. The heat will react with the lemon joice. This will make your mesage appear!

Name **Week #16**

prewrite/brainstorm

A biography is the story of a person's life. Think of someone you know and would like to write a biography about. It could be someone in your family, a friend, or a neighbor. On a separate sheet of paper, write down the answers to the questions on the right.

1. Where and when was this person born?
2. What were the family and home of this person like?
3. Where did this person go to school?
4. What jobs has this person had?
5. What special interests, hobbies, sports, or crafts does this person enjoy?
6. What interesting things have happened to this person?

Day #1

draft

Continue working on the biography. Look at the answers you wrote for the six questions. Now, draft a paragraph about that person using the information. Include a topic sentence and a conclusion.

____

____

____

____

Day #2

revise

Read what you wrote yesterday. Can you be more specific? Do you have information that does not support your topic sentence? Do you need to change your sentence order? Rewrite your ideas in a new paragraph. Change nouns, verbs, and adjectives to more specific words.

____

____

____

Day #3

proofread

Proofread your new paragraph. Are any words misspelled? Did you use the correct verb form? Make sure your capitalization and punctuation are correct. Mark the corrections with proofreading marks.

- ❒ ✓ Capitalization Mistakes
- ❒ ✓ Odd Grammar
- ❒ ✓ Punctuation Mistakes
- ❒ ✓ Spelling Mistakes

Day #4

Assessment

Assessment #16

publish

Now it is time to publish your writing. Write your final copy on the lines below.
MAKE SURE it turns out:

- NEAT—Make sure there are no wrinkles, creases, or holes.
- CLEAN—Erase any smudges or dirty spots.
- EASY TO READ—Use your best handwriting and good spacing between words.

Name

Week # 17

Day #1

Circle the choice that shows the right capitalization.

1. a. tuesday, january 22
   b. tuesday, January 22
   c. Tuesday, January 22

Circle the correct word.

2. (He, Him) and Brenda are (hour, our) cousins.

Mark the sentence to add the missing punctuation.

3. Kathy and Leopold entered the capsule

Circle the correct word for the sentence.

4. My dad (lies, lays) in the hammock for hours.

Day #2

Circle the choice that shows the right capitalization.

1. a. Our teacher is mr. Coviak.
   b. Our Teacher is Mr. Coviak.
   c. Our teacher is Mr. Coviak.

Circle the correct word.

2. (Affects/Effects) of the earthquake can be seen everywhere (accept, except) the shelter.

Mark the sentence to add the missing punctuation.

3. What is their mission

Circle the correct word for the sentence.

4. Mike has (lain, laid) his scissors on the desk.

Day #3

Circle the choice that shows the right capitalization.

1. a. *The house on the hill*
   b. *The House on the Hill*
   c. *The House On the Hill*

Circle the correct word.

2. Every one of the (us, we) boys passed (their, his) test.

Mark the sentence to add the missing punctuation.

3. Look out It's an asteroid

Circle the correct word for the sentence.

4. The papers have (laid, lain) on the desk for weeks.

Day #4

Circle the choice that shows the right capitalization.

1. a. Police Chief Harry Martinez
   b. Police Chief Harry martinez
   c. Police chief Harry Martinez

Circle the correct word.

2. Dorene and (I, me) helped Wanda with (she, her) homework.

Mark the sentence to add the missing punctuation.

3. Kathy calls back to the ship

Circle the correct word for the sentence.

4. (Lay, Lie) down, Spot!

Assessment

Assessment # 17

Circle the choices that show the right capitalization.

1. a. *Fire marshall Penny Young*
   b. *Fire Marshall Penny Young*
   c. *fire marshall Penny Young*

2. a. *My Dog is from Pluto*
   b. *My dog Is from pluto*
   c. *My Dog Is from Pluto*

3. a. *Is Mr. Brown your Teacher?*
   b. *Is mr. Brown your teacher?*
   c. *Is Mr. Brown your teacher?*

Circle the correct word.

4. Richard and (she, her) did well in every subject (accept, except) history.
5. Uncle Bill thanked (us, we) children for (hour, our) concern.

Mark the sentences to add the missing punctuation.

6. They are on their way into deep space
7. Before the launch, they checked their seat belts
8. How long will it take them to get to the moon

Circle the correct word for the sentence.

9. The lion (lies, lays) quietly, waiting for its prey.
10. You can (lie, lay) your coat on the chair.

Name Week # 18

prewrite/brainstorm

In order to do anything—make a cake or give your dog a bath—you have to carry out a number of steps in the right order, or sequence. How do you make your favorite sandwich? For prewriting, make a list of the steps you take when you build your favorite sandwich.

____
____
____
____

Day #1

draft

Write a paragraph about how to make your favorite sandwich. Use words like *first, next, then,* and *finally* to help show the right order.

____
____
____
____

Day #2

revise

Look at your draft. Did you begin with a sentence explaining what the paragraph is about? Did you put the sequence in the right order? Did you use words like *first, next, then,* and *finally* to help show the right order?

____
____
____
____

Day #3

proofread

Proofread your new paragraph. Are any words misspelled? Did you use the correct verb form? Make sure your capitalization and punctuation are correct. Mark the corrections with proofreading marks.

- ❐ ✓ Capitalization Mistakes
- ❐ ✓ Odd Grammar
- ❐ ✓ Punctuation Mistakes
- ❐ ✓ Spelling Mistakes

Day #4

Assessment

Assessment # 18

publish

Now it is time to publish your writing. Write your final copy on the lines below.

MAKE SURE it turns out:

- NEAT—Make sure there are no wrinkles, creases, or holes.
- CLEAN—Erase any smudges or dirty spots.
- EASY TO READ—Use your best handwriting and good spacing between words.

0-7682-3225-2 *Write 4 Today*

Name

Week # 19

Day #1

Underline with three short lines the first letter of words that need to be capitalized.

1. last may i wrote a poem called "oodles of noodles."

Draw a line under the complete subject. Circle the simple subject.

2. The tired kitten curled up in front of the warm fireplace.

Add quotation marks and other punctuation where necessary in the sentence.

3. The title of my new poem is By the Seaside

Homonyms are words that sound alike but have different meanings and spellings. Circle the correct words in the sentence.

4. When did Lena (sow so sew) that (knew new) dress?

Day #2

Underline with three short lines the first letter of words that need to be capitalized.

1. when we flew to texas, terry read the entire *skater's world* magazine.

Draw a line under the complete subject. Circle the simple subject.

2. Nancy washed the dishes after lunch.

Add quotation marks and other punctuation where necessary in the sentence.

3. Does your brother still receive *Sesame Street Magazine*

Circle the correct words in the sentence.

4. Karen went to (see sea) the (principal principle).

Day #3

Underline with three short lines the first letter of words that need to be capitalized.

1. gilbert and i read a book called *east of willow creek*.

Draw a line under the complete subject. Circle the simple subject.

2. That tall boy might become a good basketball player.

Add quotation marks and other punctuation where necessary in the sentence.

3. Our Battle of the Books team won said Lisa because we all read *Holes* and *Maniac Magee*

Circle the correct words in the sentence.

4. Use good (stationary stationery) to (right write rite) your letter.

Day #4

Underline with three short lines the first letter of words that need to be capitalized.

1. joseph wrote for the rutgers university newspaper *the daily targum*.

Draw a line under the complete subject. Circle the simple subject.

2. The billowing black smoke could be seen for miles.

Add quotation marks and other punctuation where necessary in the sentence.

3. Keesha your dogs collar needs to be replaced

Circle the correct words in the sentence.

4. Yolanda drew a (strait straight) line across that (piece peace) of (would wood).

Assessment

Assessment #19

Using proofreading marks, mark the first letter of words that need to be capitalized and add punctuation to the sentences.

1. i read the book *little women* in the fifth grade
2. maria wrote a poem called my favorite friend and i
3. dad, do you like the magazine *sports illustrated*
4. grandmas favorite magazine is *family circle*

Draw a line under the complete subject. Circle the simple subject.

5. Pretty pink streamers hung from the ceiling.
6. The cool night air felt good after a long, hot day.
7. The large spider plant hung over the patio entrance.

Circle the correct words in the sentences.

8. Juan threw a pair of (knew new) skates (right write) over the fence.
9. Can you (sea see) if this picture is hanging (straight strait)?
10. Jai gave the (principal principle) a (piece peace) of birthday cake.

Name

Week # 20

prewrite/brainstorm

Day #1

A good way to support the topic sentence of your writing is by providing examples. Read the topic sentence in the word web below and fill in examples that support it.

Countless animals can make great indoor pets.

draft

Day #2

Using the examples you created in the word web, draft a paragraph. Begin with the topic sentence, then write about at least three supporting examples.

____

____

____

____

____

revise

Day #3

Look at the paragraph you wrote about pets. Did you begin with a sentence that introduces the topic? Did you write at least three supporting examples and use transition words to help the reader move from one idea to the next? Rewrite the paragraph.

____

____

____

____

proofread

Day #4

Proofread your paragraph that gives examples of indoor pets. Are any words misspelled? Did you use the correct verb form? Make sure your capitalization and punctuation are correct. Mark the corrections with proofreading marks.

- ❐ ✓ Capitalization Mistakes
- ❐ ✓ Odd Grammar
- ❐ ✓ Punctuation Mistakes
- ❐ ✓ Spelling Mistakes

Assessment # 20

publish

Now it is time to publish your writing. Write your final copy on the lines below.

MAKE SURE it turns out:

- NEAT—Make sure there are no wrinkles, creases, or holes.
- CLEAN—Erase any smudges or dirty spots.
- EASY TO READ—Use your best handwriting and good spacing between words.

Name

Week # 21

Day #1

Use proofreading marks to correct the capitalization mistakes in the sentence.

1. on october 3, we had a Birthday Party!

Circle the correct verb in the sentence.

2. Tamishka (was/were) 12 years old.

Using proofreading marks, add the missing punctuation to the sentence.

3. Did you know she was that old

Circle the correct word in the sentence.

4. (Their/There/They're) were fifteen people at the party.

Day #2

Use proofreading marks to correct the capitalization mistakes in the sentence.

1. the Basketball Games in march were exciting!

Circle the correct verb in the sentence.

2. The players (was/were) happy when they won the trophy.

Using proofreading marks, add the missing punctuation to the sentence.

3. The next day they bought a case for the trophy

Circle the correct word in the sentence.

4. (Their/There/They're) trophy is in the school gymnasium.

Day #3

Use proofreading marks to correct the capitalization mistake in the sentence.

1. Have you ever visited a different State?

Circle the correct verb in the sentence.

2. The beginning of our vacation (was/were) very busy.

Using proofreading marks, add the missing punctuation to the sentence.

3. My family visited Milwaukee Wisconsin and Indianapolis Indiana.

Circle the correct verb in the sentence.

4. We like Wisconsin because (it's/its) very green and hilly!

Day #4

Use proofreading marks to correct the capitalization mistakes in the sentence.

1. my friend Sally and her Cousin tabitha ate lunch together.

Circle the correct verb in the sentence.

2. Sally said the soup (was/were) delicious.

Using proofreading marks, add the missing punctuation to the sentence.

3. Sally asked her mother what she put in the soup

Circle the correct verb in the sentence.

4. Her mother said, "(Its/It's) a secret!"

Assessment

Assessment # 21

Use proofreading marks to fix the mistakes in the ten sentences. Look for spelling, capitalization, punctuation, and grammar mistakes.

1. The Pilgrims sailed from Plymouth England on the *Mayflower* on september 6, 1620.
2. They're was 102 passengers on board.
3. the beginning of the voyage were pleasant, but then the ship ran into storms and high winds.
4. Beams on deck was cracking and letting water leak into the ship
5. Two adults died on the voyage, and one baby named "oceanus" were born.
6. On november 9, 1620, the Mayflower neared it's destination—land!
7. It were where Cape Cod Massachusetts is now.
8. Two days later, after 66 days at sea, the ship dropped it's anchor
9. Some of the Pilgrims went ashore to check out there new home
10. Now we remember there first harvest Celebration on Thanksgiving Day.

Name

Week # 22

prewrite/brainstorm

Authors have a reason for writing: they want to entertain, inform, or persuade the reader. In persuasion, the writer wants to persuade the reader to do something or think a certain way. Begin to create a persuasive paragraph. First, list the reasons you think your father should take you to the library.

Day #1

draft

Using your list of reasons to go to the library, draft a paragraph to persuade your father to take you to the library. Remember to include a topic sentence and a concluding sentence.

Day #2

revise

Look at your rough draft. Is it persuasive? Does it have a topic sentence? Does it have points that fit your topic sentence? Did you write a concluding sentence? Rewrite your paragraph, and make your words more specific.

Day #3

proofread

Now it's time to proofread your persuasive paragraph. Look at your final paragraph. Are all of the words spelled correctly? Did you capitalize words that need to be capitalized? Did you use the correct verbs and nouns? Proofread your paragraph.

- ❒ ✓ Capitalization Mistakes
- ❒ ✓ Odd Grammar
- ❒ ✓ Punctuation Mistakes
- ❒ ✓ Spelling Mistakes

Day #4

Name

Assessment # 22

Assessment

publish

Now it is time to publish your writing. Write yo final copy on the lines bel .

MAKE SURE it turns out:

- NEAT—Make sure there are no wrinkles, eases, or holes.
- CLEAN—Erase any smudges or dirty spo
- EASY TO READ—Use your best handwriti and good spacing between words.

Name

Week # 23

Day #1

Circle the choice that shows the right capitalization.

1. a. *Harriet The Spy*
   b. *Harriet the Spy*
   c. *Harriet The spy*

Write a possessive pronoun that could replace the boldfaced word.

2. ________________ **Bryan's** dog is a basset hound.

Use a semicolon to combine the two independent clauses into a compound sentence.

3. The Olympic games originated in ancient Greece. They were held from 776 B.C. to A.D. 393.

____

____

Cross out the incorrect reflexive pronoun. Write it correctly on the line.

4. Today I made meself dinner. ________________

Day #2

Circle the choice that shows the right capitalization.

1. a. *Julie of The Wolves*
   b. *Julie Of The Wolves*
   c. *Julie of the Wolves*

Write a possessive pronoun that could replace the boldfaced words.

2. ________________ **The dog's** legs are short and stocky.

Use a semicolon to combine the two independent clauses into a compound sentence.

3. The Olympic Games were held every fourth summer. The games were held at Olympia in honor of Zeus.

____

____

Cross out the incorrect reflexive pronoun. Write it correctly on the line.

4. Tim and Judy timed theirself running one mile. ________________

Day #3

Circle the choice that shows the right capitalization.

1. a. *The Boxcar children*
   b. *The Boxcar Children*
   c. *the Boxcar children*

Write a possessive pronoun that could replace the boldfaced words.

2. ________________ **Kenny's and my** bedroom has bunk beds.

Use a semicolon to combine the two independent clauses into a compound sentence.

3. Women were forbidden to compete in and watch the Olympics. They held their own games called the Heraea. ________________

____

Cross out the incorrect reflexive pronoun. Write it correctly on the line.

4. The coach wrote hisself a note to remember snacks. ________________

Day #4

Circle the choice that shows the right capitalization.

1. a. *the Indian in the Cupboard*
   b. *The Indian in the Cupboard*
   c. *The Indian in The Cupboard*

Write a possessive pronoun that could replace the boldfaced words.

2. ________________ The picture of the sunset is **the Sandovals'**.

Use a semicolon to combine the two independent clauses into a compound sentence.

3. The women's games were held every four years. There were fewer events.

____

____

Cross out the incorrect reflexive pronoun. Write it correctly on the line.

4. After we won the game, we gave ourself a pat on the back. ________________

Assessment

Assessment # 23

Circle the choice that shows the right capitalization.

1. a. *the chocolate Touch*
   b. *The Chocolate touch*
   c. *The Chocolate Touch*
2. a. *The Case of the Muttering Mummy*
   b. *The Case of The Muttering Mummy*
   c. *The Case Of the Muttering Mummy*

For each problem, write a possessive pronoun that could replace the boldfaced words.

3. ____________________ That jacket is **Mr. Yeager's**.
4. ____________________ **The Washingtons'** house is on Maple Avenue.
5. ____________________ That is **Rosie's and my** teacher.

Use a semicolon to combine the two independent clauses into a compound sentence.

6. The winners were crowned with chaplets of wild olive. Their home city-states also awarded valuable gifts and privileges to the champions.

   ____

   ____

7. Discus throw was a popular event with the ancient Greeks. The champion was considered the greatest athlete.

   ____

   ____

Rewrite the sentences correctly, using the proper reflexive pronoun.

8. The boy did the dishes by hisselves.

   ____

9. How could we move the car by ourself?

   ____

10. The cats almost injured theirself when they jumped out of the tree.

    ____

Name **Week # 24**

prewrite/brainstorm

News stories contain specific facts that explain the five Ws. Pick one of the headlines below. Circle it; then make up a list that explains the five W's.

Sioux City Disc Jockey Plays Music from Helicopter / New Science Museum to Open

Who? ______________________

What? ______________________

When? ______________________

Where? ______________________

Why? ______________________

draft

Write a news story that explains the headline. Begin your story with a lead. A lead gives the important facts and is interesting, so the reader will continue to read the news story. Be sure to include your five W's.

____

____

____

____

revise

Read your news story. Did you include all five W's? Is the most important fact in the beginning of your story? Is the least important fact at the end? Did you use transition words between sentences? Rewrite the story.

____

____

____

____

proofread

Look at your news story. Are all of the words spelled correctly? Did you capitalize words that need to be capitalized? Did you use the correct verbs and nouns? Proofread your story to make sure it is correct.

❒ ✓ Capitalization Mistakes

❒ ✓ Odd Grammar

❒ ✓ Punctuation Mistakes

❒ ✓ Spelling Mistakes

Day #2

Day #3

Day #4

Assessment # 24

publish

Now it is time to publish your writing. Write your final copy on the lines below.

MAKE SURE it turns out:

- NEAT—Make sure there are no wrinkles, creases, or holes.
- CLEAN—Erase any smudges or dirty spots.
- EASY TO READ—Use your best handwriting and good spacing between words.

Name **Week #25**

Using proofreading marks, correct the capitalization errors in the sentence.

1. Today dad and i are going to the Park.

Circle the correct word in the sentence.

2. (Its/It's) the Great Junkyard Racecar Day!

Write the missing apostrophe in the sentence. On the line, write the two words that make up the contraction or write **no contractions** if the sentence has none.

3. The fifth graders racecars had to be built using junk. ______________________

Using proofreading marks, correct the spelling error in the sentence.

4. I can't weight to see whose racing first!

Day #1

Using proofreading marks, correct the capitalization errors in the sentence.

1. the first group to race will be benjamin's Group.

Circle the correct word in the sentence.

2. My favorite teacher, Ms. Dreyden, was (their/there/they're), too.

Write the missing apostrophe in the sentence. On the line, write the two words that make up the contraction or write **no contractions** if the sentence has none.

3. Oh, no! The cars wheels fell off. Thats too bad. ______________________

Using proofreading marks, correct the spelling error in the sentence.

4. Witch car is your favourite?

Day #2

Using proofreading marks, correct the capitalization errors in the sentence.

1. Wow, Mrs. nelson's Kindergarten class is at the race, too.

Circle the correct word in the sentence.

2. Isn't that (your/you're) sister over there?

Write the missing apostrophe in the sentence. On the line, write the two words that make up the contraction or write **no contractions** if the sentence has none.

3. It looks like theyre making repairs to the cars front end. ______________________

Using proofreading marks, correct the spelling errors in the sentence.

4. That's becuz the car is going to fall a part.

Day #3

Using proofreading marks, correct the capitalization errors in the sentence.

1. did you see mr. Garcia's red car in the race?

Circle the correct word in the sentence.

2. (Its/It's) the fastest car in the race.

Write the missing apostrophe in the sentence. On the line, write the two words that make up the contraction or write **no contractions** if the sentence has none.

3. Im going to build the fastest car for next years race. ______________________

Using proofreading marks, correct the spelling errors in the sentence.

4. Mom was pleazed and surprized that my sister's car stayed in one peace.

Day #4

Assessment

Assessment # 25

Use proofreading marks to fix the ten mistakes in the letter below. Look for spelling, capitalization, punctuation, and grammar mistakes.

9545 Bay View Lane

Dublin, Ohio

October 22, 2004

Dear Grandma and Grandpa,

I wanted to write to tell you about Buster. He's my new puppy! Busters fur is black, and his ears are pointed. Hes always sniffing around. He likes chasing ducks at the Pond. They get so mad at him! Buster wants to play all the time, and he loves being outside. Right now, dad is giving Buster a bath...in tomato juice! Thats what we had to use becuz he surprized a skunk in our yard. Mom says the juice will take out the skunk smell. I sure hope so! Please write and tell me how your doing. I can barely weight for your visit here next month.

You're grandson,

Alex

Name

Week # 27

Using proofreading marks, correct the capitalization errors in the sentence.

1. my Cousin will graduate from sullivan high school on june 19, 2006.

Circle the correct words in the sentence.

2. He is the (most funniest funniest) comedian I have ever heard.

Using proofreading marks, correct the punctuation errors in the sentence.

3. Dr. Jacobs Mr. W. Allen Jr. and Father co-own that building.

Circle the correct word in the sentence.

4. Jimmy, please put the groceries over (hear/here).

Using proofreading marks, correct the capitalization errors in the sentence.

1. Stain Free Cleaning company transferred you to texas, right, dad?

Circle the correct words in the sentence.

2. Today's game was (more better better) than yesterday's.

Using proofreading marks, correct the punctuation errors in the sentence.

3. Eddie that tall dark and handsome young man plays golf his brother plays tennis

Circle the correct word in the sentence.

4. (Principal/Principle) Hillary said my brother learned a lesson.

Using proofreading marks, correct the capitalization errors in the sentence.

1. did principal rodgers tell you that history I is now meeting in room 8?

Circle the correct words in the sentence.

2. That dress is the (prettier prettiest) of the two.

Using proofreading marks, correct the punctuation errors in the sentence.

3. Yes Emily I did buy tissues but I forgot the box of green tea" mother said

Circle the correct word in the sentence.

4. The (ball/bawl) flew right through Mrs. Diego's window.

Day #3

Using proofreading marks, correct the capitalization errors in the sentence.

1. the Smith Family asked for twenty-five dollars worth of Gasoline.

Circle the correct words in the sentence.

2. Andrea is the (more friendly most friendly) girl in the class.

Using proofreading marks, correct the punctuation errors in the sentence.

3. Father will I believe arrive on the 9 15 train

Circle the correct word in the sentence.

4. I didn't know Jamie went (threw/through) the training program.

Day #4

Assessment

Assessment # 27

Using proofreading marks, correct the capitalization and punctuation errors in the sentences.

1. nancy your april beauty magazine has arrived said her Sister

2. yes we re going to see a Play with our literature II class

3. where did you say you were going Sam

4. the Anderson Family lives near hope high school

5. Quick Printing company printed the posters flyers and cards for our Sale

Circle the correct form of adjective in the sentence.

6. Who is the (louder loudest) person in class?

7. Harry is the (quietest quieter) person I've ever met.

8. That old barn is the (tallest taller) building in the neighborhood.

Circle the correct words in the sentences.

9. My sister got a (bawl/ball) for her fifth birthday.

10. "This summer was great!" said (Principle/Principal) Jones.

Name **Week # 28**

prewrite/brainstorm

A movie review gives the writer's opinion of a movie. Think about a movie you have seen recently. How would you rate it? Brainstorm and make a list of your opinions about the movie. What did or didn't you like? Was it exciting or scary? Did it make you laugh or cry? What was your favorite part? Would you recommend it?

Day #1

draft

Write a movie review based on your list that describes your opinion of the movie. Be sure to include a topic sentence that states the movie's name and explains your opinion. Conclude your review with your recommendation.

Day #2

revise

Read your movie review. Does the review begin in an interesting way? Will the reader understand what the movie is about? Is your opinion of the movie clear? Rewrite the review with more specific words.

Day #3

proofread

Proofread your movie review. Are any words misspelled? Did you use the correct verb form? Did you use proper capitalization and punctuation for the movie title? Make sure all your capitalization and punctuation are correct. Mark the corrections with proofreading marks.

- ❒ ✓ Capitalization Mistakes
- ❒ ✓ Odd Grammar
- ❒ ✓ Punctuation Mistakes
- ❒ ✓ Spelling Mistakes

Day #4

Assessment # 28

publish

Now it is time to publish your writing. Write your final copy on the lines below.

MAKE SURE it turns out:

- NEAT—Make sure there are no wrinkles, creases, or holes.
- CLEAN—Erase any smudges or dirty spots.
- EASY TO READ—Use your best handwriting and good spacing between words.

Name

Week # 29

Day #1

Use proofreading marks to correct the capitalization error(s) in the sentence.

1. bobby smith and rachel andrews are in the same class.

Write the correct demonstrative pronoun to complete the sentence.

2. I am not wearing my glasses. Can you read _________ note for me?

Use proofreading marks to add the missing quotation marks and comma(s).

3. The Golden Gate Bridge is one of the largest suspension bridges in the world said Mr. Yu.

Fill in the circle next to the correct verb to complete the sentence.

4. We have to _________ up two more rows of chairs.
   ❍ sit ❍ set

Day #2

Use proofreading marks to correct the capitalization error(s) in the sentence.

1. Her aunt is lieutenant colonel Eleanor Cooghan.

Write the correct demonstrative pronoun to complete the sentence.

2. Mammals are warm-blooded. _________ is a fact.

Use proofreading marks to add the missing quotation marks and comma(s).

3. Exactly how long is the bridge? asked Davida.

Fill in the circle next to the correct verb to complete the sentence.

4. The sun will _________ tonight at 7:25 p.m.
   ❍ set ❍ sit

Day #3

Use proofreading marks to correct the capitalization error(s) in the sentence.

1. Do you know governor jordan of South dakota?

Write the correct demonstrative pronoun to complete the sentence.

2. The trees by the creek are huge. But _________ across the street are small.

Use proofreading marks to add the missing quotation marks and comma(s).

3. The bridge is 8,981 feet long Mr. Yu answered and is in California.

Fill in the circle next to the correct verb to complete the sentence.

4. Logan, please _________ down.
   ❍ sit ❍ set

Day #4

Use proofreading marks to correct the capitalization error(s) in the sentence.

1. Hey, dad, remember that I have Football practice after school today.

Write the correct demonstrative pronoun to complete the sentence.

2. "I like your earrings." "Thanks, my mom bought _________ for my birthday."

Use proofreading marks to add the missing quotation marks and comma(s).

3. Mr. Yu continued The bridge has always been painted orange.

Fill in the circle next to the correct verb to complete the sentence.

4. Why don't you _________ over there?
   ❍ sit ❍ set

Assessm[illegible]ent # 29

Use proofrea[illegible]ing marks to correct the capitalization errors in the sentences.

1. the princi[illegible]l of their School is mr. wesley schmidt.
2. on Friday, [illegible] class is going to judge sanchez's Courtroom.

Write the correc[illegible] demonstrative pronoun to complete the sentence.

3. Who donate[illegible] the canned goods for the shelter? Jose donated __________.
4. Mom picked [illegible] the racecar. "Where did you get __________?" she asked.
5. Clayton's sister [illegible]ok his baseball glove. "Give me __________!" Clayton yelled.

Use proofreading m[illegible]s to add the missing quotation marks and commas.

6. Why is the bridge [illegible]med Golden Gate, when its color is orange asked Marta.
7. Mr. Yu explained A[illegible]ually, the term 'Golden Gate' refers to the Golden Gate Strait, the entrance [illegible] the San Francisco Bay from the Pacific Ocean.
8. Construction on the [illegible]dge began on January 5, 1933, and the bridge was opened on May 28, [illegible]7 said Mr. Yu.

Fill in the circle next to the [illegible]rrect verb to complete the sentence.

9. _____ the basket of groc[illegible]es on the table.

   ❍ Sit ❍ Se[illegible]

10. Anna usually _____ at the [illegible]ad of the table.

    ❍ sits ❍ sets

Name **Week # 30**

prewrite/brainstorm

A paragraph that tells how things are the same or different is called a compare-and-contrast paragraph. Using the Venn diagram, write your ideas about how living in the city is different or the same as living in the country.

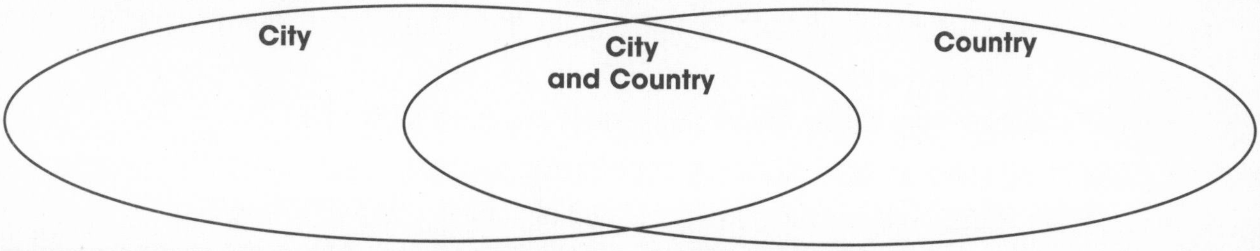

Day #1

draft

Use the information you wrote in the Venn diagram to write a compare-and-contrast paragraph about living in the city or country. Remember to include a topic sentence and a conclusion statement.

Day #2

revise

Look at your draft. Did you begin with a topic sentence? Did you use specific words to describe similarities and differences? Did you use a conclusion sentence? Rewrite your paragraph with more specific words.

Day #3

proofread

Finally, proofread your compare-and-contrast paragraph. Are all of the words spelled correctly? Did you capitalize words that need to be capitalized? Did you use the correct verbs and nouns? Make proofreading marks in your paragraph.

- ❒ ✓ Capitalization Mistakes
- ❒ ✓ Odd Grammar
- ❒ ✓ Punctuation Mistakes
- ❒ ✓ Spelling Mistakes

Day #4

Assessment

Assessment # 30

publish

Now it is time to publish your writing. Write your final copy on the lines below.

MAKE SURE it turns out:

- NEAT—Make sure there are no wrinkles, creases, or holes.
- CLEAN—Erase any smudges or dirty spots.
- EASY TO READ—Use your best handwriting and good spacing between words.

Name

Week # 31

Day #1

Fill in the circle next to the word that is capitalized correctly.

1. Cathie speaks _________ fluently.
   ❍ italian ❍ Italian

Write three adjectives that describe the noun.

2. kitten ______________________________

Add the missing quotation marks around the title of the short work in the sentence.

3. Did you read The City's Top Teacher article in the local newspaper?

Cross out the improperly spelled reflexive pronoun in the sentence. Spell it correctly on the line.

4. Mom, I hurt meself while playing crack the whip. ______________

Day #2

Fill in the circle next to the word that is capitalized correctly.

1. The _________ Olympians wore the brightest uniforms.
   ❍ canadian ❍ Canadian

Write three adjectives that describe the noun.

2. tree ______________________________

Add the missing quotation marks around the title of the short work in the sentence.

3. Have you heard Shel Silverstein's poem, Screamin' Millie?

Cross out the improperly spelled reflexive pronoun in the sentence. Spell it correctly on the line.

4. Kent bought hisself a pair of sunglasses. ______________

Day #3

Fill in the circle next to the word that is capitalized correctly.

1. Carlos passed _________ 104, but he failed _________
   ❍ astronomy ❍ Astronomy ❍ economics ❍ Economics

Write three adjectives that describe the noun.

2. chair ______________________________

Add the missing quotation marks around the title of the short work in the sentence.

3. I can't wait to get home so I can read the last chapter, The Surprise.

Cross out the improperly spelled reflexive pronoun in the sentence. Spell it correctly on the line.

4. After the victory, the baseball team treated theirself to ice cream. ______________

Day #4

Fill in the circle next to the word that is capitalized correctly.

1. Lance needs to work on his _________ irregular verbs.
   ❍ spanish ❍ Spanish

Write three adjectives that describe the noun.

2. cactus ______________________________

Add the missing quotation marks around the title of the short work in the sentence.

3. Shelly is singing The Star Spangled Banner at the hockey game on Thursday.

Cross out the improperly spelled reflexive pronoun in the sentence. Spell it correctly on the line.

4. Justin and I gave ourself a second chance to run the race. ______________

Name Week # 31

Assessment

Assessment # 31

Fill in the circle next to the word that is capitalized correctly.

1. Kellie loves _____ food.

   ❍ french ❍ French

2. Mr. Saunders teaches _____ and _____.

   ❍ journalism ❍ Journalism ❍ german ❍ German

3. Jason's mom is studying _____ literature.

   ❍ English ❍ english

Write three adjectives that describe each of the nouns.

5. cake ______________________________

6. dentist ______________________________

Add the missing quotation marks around the titles of the short works in the sentences.

6. Please give me the newspaper when you finish so I can read the article Fleeing the Flames.

7. In the article, Colonial Heroines, you will read the stories of four amazing women who changed the face of colonial America.

8. Did you hear Aaron Carter's song, Another Earthquake, on the radio?

Cross out the improperly spelled reflexive pronoun in the sentence. Write it correctly on the line.

9. The girl went to the theater by herselves. ____________________

10. How could you go water skiing by youself? ____________________

Name

Week # 32

prewrite/brainstorm

Realistic fiction is a story that could be true but isn't. It has two main purposes: to tell an interesting story and to send an important message (theme). Use the story starter to write a realistic fiction story. Read the information, and then fill in the boxes with your ideas.

Setting:

Main Characters:

Theme:

Problem:

Event 1:

Event 2:

Event 3:

Solution:

Day #1

draft

Today it's time to write your realistic fiction story. Follow the story starter you made to help you to describe the problem, the three events, and the solution.

Day #2

revise

Read your realistic fiction story. How could you improve it? Do you need to add more details? Do you need to rearrange the order of events? Rewrite your story. Be sure you use specific verbs and nouns to describe the characters and events.

Day #3

proofread

Finally, proofread your story. Are all of the words spelled correctly? Did you capitalize words that need to be capitalized? Did you use the correct verbs and nouns? Make proofreading marks in your paragraph.

- ❒ ✓ Capitalization Mistakes
- ❒ ✓ Odd Grammar
- ❒ ✓ Punctuation Mistakes
- ❒ ✓ Spelling Mistakes

Day #4

Name

Assessment # 32

publish

Now it is time to publish your writing. Write your final copy on the lines below.
MAKE SURE it turns out:

- NEAT—Make sure there are no wrinkles, creases, or holes.
- CLEAN—Erase any smudges or dirty spots.
- EASY TO READ—Use your best handwriting and good spacing between words.

Name **Week # 33**

Day #1

Use proofreading marks to correct the capitalization errors in the sentence.

1. Charles Lindbergh, the first person to fly nonstop from new york to paris, named his plane *the spirit of st. louis.*

Fill in the missing verb forms.

	Present Tense	**Past Tense**	**Past Participle** (use with has, had, or had)
2.	break	____________	____________
3.	bring	____________	____________

Add the missing commas to the sentences.

4. Julia watch me throw this clock out the window. Why Mackenzie? I want to see time fly!

Day #2

Use proofreading marks to correct the capitalization errors in the sentence.

1. The caldecott medal is awarded to the illustrator of the most distinguished children's picture book published in America.

Read the nouns in each row. Write the missing adjective and verb.

	Noun	**Adjective**	**Adverb**
2.	success	____________	____________
3.	independence	____________	____________

Add the missing commas to the sentences.

4. Hunter do you have a mirror? No Tom why? I want to see if the cat's got my tongue!

Day #3

Use proofreading marks to correct the capitalization errors in the sentence.

1. The sears tower, in chicago, illinois, has 110 stories.

Fill in the missing verb forms.

	Present Tense	**Past Tense**	**Past Participle** (use with has, had, or had)
2.	draw	____________	____________
3.	drink	____________	____________

Add the missing commas to the sentences.

4. Janey and Michelle are you sick? No we just painted our faces green!

Day #4

Use proofreading marks to correct the capitalization errors in the sentence.

1. The bill of rights is the first 10 amendments to the constitution of the united states.

Read the nouns in each row. Write the missing adjective and verb.

	Noun	**Adjective**	**Adverb**
2.	affection	____________	____________
3.	ease	____________	____________

Add the missing commas to the sentences.

4. Snort-snort! Matthew why are you snorting like a pig? Well Nicole I wanted to go hog wild!

Name

Assessment

Assessment # 33

Use proofreading marks to correct the capitalization errors in the sentence.

1. The *nina, pinta,* and *santa maria* were the three ships christopher columbus sailed on his first voyage westward.
2. Kim Dae Jung won the 2000 nobel peace prize.
3. The empire state building is taller than the john hancock center.

Fill in the missing verbs in this list of irregular past tense verbs.

	Present Tense	Past Tense	Past Participle (use with has, have, or had)
4.	get	__________	__________
	give	__________	__________
5.	hide	__________	__________
	know	__________	__________
6.	speak	__________	__________
	take	__________	__________

Add the missing commas to the sentence.

7. Will you pretend you are lightning Fernando? OK if you want me to.
8. Boy that was disgusting! Don't ever make me pay through the nose again Mrs. McCreary!

Read the nouns in each row. Write the missing adjective and adverb.

	Noun	Adjective	Adverb
9.	responsibility	__________	__________
	wisdom	__________	__________
10.	anger	__________	__________
	silence	__________	__________

Name **Week # 34**

prewrite/brainstorm

A business letter is more formal than a friendly letter. It is usually written to someone you do not know. Your message should be brief, clear, and to the point. You want to arrange a field trip to a local company. Use the list to plan your letter.

Who are you? (introduce yourself) ______________________________

Where do you want to go? ______________________________

What do you want to do? ______________________________

Why do you want to do this? ______________________________

When do you want it to happen? ______________________________

Day #1

draft

Now it's time to write your business letter. Be sure to include all of the details you wrote down on your list. On a separate sheet of paper, write a letter using the business letter form.

Day #2

revise

Read over your business letter. Does the letter explain why you want to visit the local company? Does it explain the other details from your list? Is it arranged with an introduction, the body, and a closing? Rewrite the letter on another sheet of paper to make it clearer and more specific.

Day #3

proofread

Today, proofread your business letter. Are all of the words spelled correctly? Did you capitalize words that need to be capitalized? Did you use the correct verbs and nouns? Make proofreading marks in your paragraph.

- ❒ ✓ Capitalization Mistakes
- ❒ ✓ Odd Grammar
- ❒ ✓ Punctuation Mistakes
- ❒ ✓ Spelling Mistakes

Day #4

Assessment

A sessment # 34

p blish

Now it is time to publish your writing. Write your final copy on the lines below.

MAKE SURE it turns out:

- NEAT—Make sure there are no wrinkles, creases, or holes.
- CLEAN—Erase any smudges or dirty spots.
- EASY TO READ—Use your best handwriting and good spacing between words.

0-7682-3225-2 *Write 4 Today*

Name **Week # 35**

Day #1

Use proofreading marks to correct the capitalization.

1. I am going to visit my grandparents and my aunt eleanor.

Read the sentence. Write the correct missing word on the line.

2. ______________ book is this? (Who's, Whose)

Add the missing punctuation mark and write an abbreviation to tell what kind of sentence it is: **D** (declarative), **Int** (interrogative), **Imp** (imperative), **E** (exclamatory).

3. _____ Max: Listen up, everyone
   _____ Mr. Chen: For math today, we are going outside to play games

Circle the correct word to complete the sentence.

4. Mason had to (accept/except) Eli's apology.

Day #2

Use proofreading marks to correct the capitalization.

1. Did you know that dr. matthews, my dentist, is danny's mom?

Read the sentence. Write the correct missing word on the line.

2. Is that the book ______________ reading for this month's assignment? (you're, your)

Add the missing punctuation mark and write an abbreviation to tell what kind of sentence it is: **D** (declarative), **Int** (interrogative), **Imp** (imperative), **E** (exclamatory).

3. _____ Class: Yay
   _____ Maria: What are we going to play

Circle the correct word to complete the sentence.

4. After a (thorough/through) search, we found the missing hamster.

Day #3

Use proofreading marks to correct the capitalization.

1. The United States has a president rather than a king or queen.

Read the sentence. Write the correct missing word on the line.

2. His aunt and uncle make him sleep in __________________ cupboard under the stairs, while Dudley gets two bedrooms. (they're, their)

Add the missing punctuation mark and write an abbreviation to tell what kind of sentence it is: **D** (declarative), **Int** (interrogative), **Imp** (imperative), **E** (exclamatory).

3. _____ Mr. Chen: I don't know—you will be making up the games
   _____ Kevin: How do we do that

Circle the correct word to complete the sentence.

4. Fair-weather friends are the ones who (desert/dessert) their team when it is losing.

Day #4

Use proofreading marks to correct the capitalization.

1. Jenny wrote her report on president james madison.

Read the sentence. Write the correct missing word on the line.

2. One day a letter arrives— __________________ addressed to "Mr. H. Potter, The Cupboard under the Stairs." (it's, its)

Add the missing punctuation mark and write an abbreviation to tell what kind of sentence it is: **D** (declarative), **Int** (interrogative), **Imp** (imperative), **E** (exclamatory).

3. _____ Mr. Chen: I am giving every group a box with materials and directions
   _____ Julie: That sounds great

Circle the correct word to complete the sentence.

4. I hate it when I (loose/lose) my homework!

Assessment

Assessment # 35

Use proofreading marks to correct the capitalization.

1. During the Civil War, general robert e. lee was the leader of the Southern troops.
2. Some people believe he was America's finest general ever.

Read the sentences. Write the correct missing word on each line.

3. Harry lives with his aunt and uncle and his spoiled cousin, Dudley. ____________ all really mean to Harry. (They're, Their)
4. ____________ the book's author? (Who's, Whose)
5. What is ____________ favorite part so far? (you're, your)

Add the missing punctuation mark and write an abbreviation to tell what kind of sentences these are: **D** (declarative), **Int** (interrogative), **Imp** (imperative), **E** (exclamatory).

6. _____ Maria: There's a measuring tape, a whistle, and 10 empty two-liter bottles
   _____ Julie: Look and see if there is anything else
7. _____ Yu-Chih: Here are the directions
   _____ Kevin: Read them aloud for us, Yu-Chih
   _____ Yu-Chih: Use these materials to make up a measurement relay game
8. _____ Maria: Hey, this'll be fun
   _____ Julie: Does anybody have an idea

Circle the correct word to complete the sentence.

9. For the war to stop, both sides had to (accept/except) the peace plan terms.
10. I am going to lie down—please wake me when it's time for (desert/dessert).

Name **Week # 36**

prewrite/brainstorm

Poetry is different from prose writing. Prose writing appears in sentences and paragraphs. Poetry appears in lines and stanzas. Brainstorm about the five senses to come up with a list of sensory words that describe water.

Water

Sight	Smell	Hearing	Taste	Touch
________	________	________	________	________
________	________	________	________	________
________	________	________	________	________

Day #1

draft

Stanzas divide groups of lines and are like paragraphs. Take your ideas about water and write a poem in quatrains (four lines in each stanza). For longer poems, use another piece of paper.

____

____

____

____

Day #2

revise

Read the poem you wrote about water. Are the lines broken into quatrains? Do you want the lines to rhyme? Look at each word. Are they the exact words that you want to use in your poem? Do the sensory words tell the reader what you think of water? Rewrite the poem to make it more specific.

____

____

____

____

Day #3

proofread

Today, proofread your poem. Are all of the words spelled correctly? Did you capitalize words that need to be capitalized? Did you use the correct punctuation? Make proofreading marks in your poem.

❒ ✓ Capitalization Mistakes

❒ ✓ Odd Grammar

❒ ✓ Punctuation Mistakes

❒ ✓ Spelling Mistakes

Day #4

Name

Assessment

Assessment # 36

publish

Now it is time to publish your writing. Write your final copy on the lines below.
MAKE SURE it turns out:

- NEAT—Make sure there are no wrinkles, creases, or holes.
- CLEAN—Erase any smudges or dirty spots.
- EASY TO READ—Use your best handwriting and good spacing between words.

Name

Week # 37

Day #1

Complete the sentence. Use correct capitalization.

1. The last movie I watched was called ______________________________.

Rewrite the sentence twice using the past tense and the past participle of the verb.

Todd begins swimming class today.

2. (Past Tense) ______________________________

3. (Past Participle) ______________________________

Read the sentences and find the homophone errors. Use proofreading marks to correct the errors.

4. Have you ever maid ice cream? Its easy too do if you no how.

Day #2

Complete the sentence. Use correct capitalization.

1. Some of my ancestors lived in ______________________________.

Rewrite the sentence twice using the past tense and the past participle of the verb.

She wears shorts when it is hot.

2. (Past Tense) ______________________________

3. (Past Participle) ______________________________

Read the sentences and find the homophone errors. Use proofreading marks to correct the errors.

4. My Ant Beth tot me how to make eyes cream. It's a grate activity if your board or hungry.

Day #3

Complete the sentence. Use correct capitalization.

1. My favorite holiday is ______________________________.

Rewrite the sentence twice using the past tense and the past participle of the verb.

Jamal drinks milk with breakfast.

2. (Past Tense) ______________________________

3. (Past Participle) ______________________________

Read the sentence and find the homophone errors. Use proofreading marks to correct the errors.

4. The hole project takes an our if you have the write ingredients and don't need to by them.

Day #4

Complete the sentence. Use correct capitalization.

1. The person I admire most is ______________________________.

Rewrite the sentence twice using the past tense and the past participle of the verb.

They go to school.

2. (Past Tense) ______________________________

3. (Past Participle) ______________________________

Read the sentence and find the homophone errors. Use proofreading marks to correct the errors.

4. Bee sure ewe have milk, whipping cream, sugar, and sum vanilla extract.

Assessment

Assessment # 37

Complete the sentences. Use correct capitalization.

1. My favorite book is called ____________________.
2. We went to ____________________ on vacation.
3. One of my favorite authors is ____________________.

Rewrite the sentence twice using the past tense and the past participle of the verb.

I see the snowstorm.

4. (Past Tense) ____________________
5. (Past Participle) ____________________

Jennifer flies to San Francisco.

6. (Past Tense) ____________________
7. (Past Participle) ____________________

Read the sentences and find the homophone errors. Use proofreading marks to correct the errors.

8. Your also going to need too coffee cans, crushed ice, and a hole bag of rock salt.

9. Ewe can add berries, chocolate chips, or candy to the ice cream, two.

10. With sum ordinary ingredients and my ant's recipe, you to can make your own ice cream.

0-7682-3225-2 *Write 4 Today*

Name

prewrite/brainstorm

Dialogue is the words spoken by characters in a story. Dialogue should be realistic. For example, a young child uses different words and phrases than an adult does. Think about the following situation and brainstorm about things the characters might say to each other. Make a list of your ideas on a separate sheet of paper.

A first grader asking for help from an older brother.

Day #1

draft

Write a conversation between the first grader and the older brother. Use quotation marks, commas, and end punctuation correctly.

Day #2

revise

Read over your conversation. Is it clear who is saying what? Do the words that the characters use fit their ages? Are the words written as if the characters were actually saying the words? Revise the conversation.

Day #3

proofread

Now it's time to proofread the conversation. Are all of the words spelled correctly? Did you capitalize words that need to be capitalized? Did you use the correct quotation marks, commas, and other punctuation? Mark corrections with proofreading marks.

- ❒ ✓ Capitalization Mistakes
- ❒ ✓ Odd Grammar
- ❒ ✓ Punctuation Mistakes
- ❒ ✓ Spelling Mistakes

Day #4

Assessment

Assessment # 38

publish

Now it is time to publish your writing. Write your final copy on the lines below.

MAKE SURE it turns out:

- NEAT—Make sure there are no wrinkles, creases, or holes.
- CLEAN—Erase any smudges or dirty spots.
- EASY TO READ—Use your best handwriting and good spacing between words.

0-7682-3225-2 *Write 4 Today*

Name **Week # 39**

Day #1

Use proofreading marks to correct the capitalization errors in the sentence.

1. Many types of cars, like the pacer, edsel, and gremlin, are no longer made.

Write *declarative, imperative, exclamatory,* or *interrogative* before the sentence. Add end punctuation and add periods after initials and abbreviations.

2. ____________________ Where are you going on your next vacation

Write the contractions for each pair of words.

3. you are ______________

does not ______________

Write the plural for these nouns.

4. march ______________

boy ______________

Day #2

Use proofreading marks to correct the capitalization errors in the sentence.

1. If you could attend a major sporting event, would you rather go to the super bowl, the stanley cup playoffs, or the kentucky derby?

Write *declarative, imperative, exclamatory,* or *interrogative* before the sentence. Add end punctuation and add periods after initials and abbreviations.

2. ____________________ Dr J C Brown taught at Harvard

Write the contractions for each pair of words.

3. he is ______________

could not ______________

Write the plural for these nouns.

4. church ______________

agency ______________

Day #3

Use proofreading marks to correct the capitalization errors in the sentence.

1. josh belongs to the boy scouts, pitches in little league, and was elected president of the lakeside stamp club last march.

Write *declarative, imperative, exclamatory,* or *interrogative* before the sentence. Add end punctuation and add periods after initials and abbreviations.

2. ____________________ Sgt Burns, go to the colonel's office

Write the contractions for each pair of words.

3. they were ______________

was not ______________

Write the plural for these nouns.

4. sketch ______________

jelly ______________

Day #4

Use proofreading marks to correct the capitalization errors in the sentence.

1. independence day, presidents day, memorial day, labor day, and christmas are all holidays.

Write *declarative, imperative, exclamatory,* or *interrogative* before the sentence. Add end punctuation and add periods after initials and abbreviations.

2. ____________________ Always be on time

Write the contractions for each pair of words.

3. you have ______________

is not ______________

Write the plural for these nouns.

4. fox ______________

family ______________

Assessment

Assessment # 39

Use proofreading marks to correct the capitalization errors in the sentence.

1. The students were given a choice of writing about the revolutionary war, the reconstruction era, the industrial revolution, or the civil war as topics for their history reports.

2. In january, i got to go on a tour of the general electric headquarters in new york city.

Write *declarative, imperative, exclamatory,* or *interrogative* before each sentence. Add end punctuation and add periods after initials and abbreviations.

3. ____________________ Don't slam the door when you leave
4. ____________________ Grandmother asked me to help her on Tuesday
5. ____________________ Was U S Grant a popular president

Write the contractions for each pair of words.

6. you are ______________ they were ______________
7. does not ______________ could not ______________
8. you have ______________ he is ______________

Write the plural for these nouns.

9. march ______________ church ______________
10. agency ______________ family ______________

Name

Week # 40

prewrite/brainstorm

When fiction writers select a narrator to tell the story, they choose a point of view. First-person narrators use I/me/my pronouns. Third-person narrators use he/she or the character's name. On the lines below, list some things that happen when you take your pet to the veterinarian.

Day #1

draft

Using the first-person point of view, write a short paragraph about taking a pet to the veterinarian. Next, write the same information in another short paragraph using third-person narration.

Day #2

revise

Today, revise your two paragraphs told from two points of view. Is the point of view clear in each paragraph? How does the reader know what the point of view is? Rewrite each paragraph, using more specific nouns and verbs.

Day #3

proofread

Now it's time to proofread the two paragraphs. Are all of the words spelled correctly? Did you capitalize words that need to be capitalized? Did you use correct punctuation? Make proofreading marks in your paragraph.

- ❐ ✓ Capitalization Mistakes
- ❐ ✓ Odd Grammar
- ❐ ✓ Punctuation Mistakes
- ❐ ✓ Spelling Mistakes

Day #4

Name

Assessment

Assessment #40

publish

Now it is time to publish your writing. Write your final copy on the lines below.

MAKE SURE it turns out:

- NEAT—Make sure there are no wrinkles, creases, or holes.
- CLEAN—Erase any smudges or dirty spots.
- EASY TO READ—Use your best handwriting and good spacing between words.

0-7682-3225-2 *Write 4 Today*

Answer Key

Name **Week #5**

Day #1

Underline with three short lines the first letter of each word that should be capitalized.

1. on december 7, 1941, the japanese attacked pearl harbor.

Read the sentences. Choose the sentence in which the subject and verb agree.

2. a. The daffodils is all blooming on the hillside.
   b. A gentle rain wash the drowsiness from the waking earth.
   (c) Seedlings wake from their long sleep.

Use proofreading marks to correct the punctuation.

3. After all of that we still didn't know how Eduardo would get to Johns game

Choose the correct spelling.

4. a. brot b. broght (c) brought d. brougth

Day #2

Underline with three short lines the first letter of each word that should be capitalized.

1. our old house was in central city, kansas.

Read the sentences. Choose the sentence in which the subject and verb agree.

2. (a) My mother worries that her garden will not grow.
   b. Dad say that this autumn we should have a good harvest.
   c. Along the riverbank, my brothers hunts for frogs.

Use proofreading marks to correct the punctuation.

3. Cinderella do you want to go to the ball now asked her fairy godmother

Choose the correct spelling.

4. (a) because b. becuz c. becaus d. becuse

Day #3

Underline with three short lines the first letter of each word that should be capitalized.

1. "could we please," carl asked mr. chen, "have some ice cream?"

Read the sentences. Choose the sentence in which the subject and verb agree.

2. a. The plow and the oxen stands ready to plant another crop.
   (b) Our coop is full of squawking chickens and crowing roosters.
   c. In the pigpen, hogs searches for their morning food.

Use proofreading marks to correct the punctuation.

3. Our teacher moved here from Bangor Maine on August 4 2002

Choose the correct spelling.

4. Kyle ______ want to play. a. didnt b. did'nt c. didnt' (d) didn't

Day #4

Underline with three short lines the first letter of each word that should be capitalized.

1. dr. shard said, "come by my office on tuesday."

Read the sentences. Choose the sentence in which the subject and verb agree.

2. (a) Before the winter came, we harvested our crops.
   b. We'll plants beans next year.
   c. Our crops fills four wagons.

Use proofreading marks to correct the punctuation.

3. Mayor Hill said Please, think about it

Choose the correct spelling.

4. Shantal loves to go to the library with her ______. a. familie b. faimily c. familee (d) family

Published by Frank Schaffer Publications. Copyright protected. 21 0-7682-3225-2 *Write 4 Today*

Name **Week #5**

Assessment #5

Certain words or phrases must be capitalized. Choose the sentence that shows the correct capitalization.

1. a. Mrs. Small moved here from san francisco, California.
   b. It was written by a very talented author named lois lowry.
   c. Dad said, "that book is fascinating."
   (d) Mom gave me a copy of the book for my birthday on May 1.
2. (a) The geese remind me of life in Canada.
   b. Le asked Hope, "will you go to Texas for vacation?"
   c. Our neighbor, mr. Kaminski, is very kind.
   d. When I grow up, I want to write a book like the harry potter books.

Read each sentence. Circle the form of the verb that agrees with the subject.

3. In the morning, we (has, **(have)**) to feed the horses, chickens, and hogs.
4. Dad (leave, **(leaves)**) after breakfast and (work, **(works)**) in the fields all day.
5. All of the household chores (**(are)** is) finished by noon.

Use proofreading marks to correct the punctuation.

6. Shanti called Ahmal and said can you travel with me and my family"
7. Charlene cant you find the golden necklace you bought in Dallas Texas?

Choose the sentence with no spelling mistakes.

8. a. The pond rippled becuz of the breeze.
   b. We broght our brand new fishing poles with us.
   c. The worms we brougth made excellent bait!
   (d) We baited our hooks and brought our lines over to the pond.
9. a. It didnt take long before my brother felt a tug.
   b. He slowly brot the line in, pulling aginst the fish.
   (c) Because the fish was strong, it made him work hard!
   d. A few rainbow trout would make a great dinner for our falmily!
10. a. Mom showed us how to clean fish so she didnt' have to do it alone.
    (b) Dad didn't mind teaching us the right way to cook them.
    c. The whole familie sat down to a delicious meal.
    d. Today was my favorite familee fishing day ever!

Published by Frank Schaffer Publications. Copyright protected. 22 0-7682-3225-2 *Write 4 Today*

Name **Week #6**

Day #1

prewrite/brainstorm

In week #4 you wrote the topic paragraph of an essay. To continue writing your multi-paragraph essay, you must decide what you want to write in your supporting paragraph. On a separate sheet of paper, draw a clustering map. Write your topic (week #4) in the middle circle. Now, brainstorm and add as many branches as you wish.

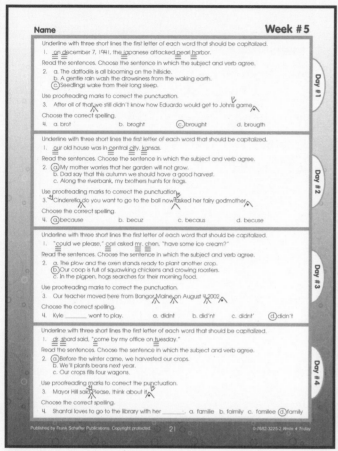

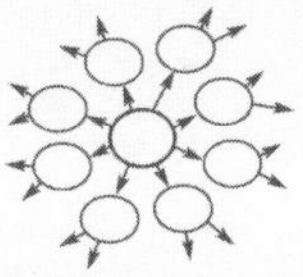

The brainstorming activity should contain various ideas or words related to the topic.

Day #2

draft

Now draft the supporting paragraph. Write about one idea that supports your topic. Use the ideas you created when you brainstormed to help you.

The first draft should contain ideas taken from the brainstorming activity.

Day #3

revise

Read what you wrote yesterday. Can you be more specific? Do you need to put your sentences in a different order? Rewrite your ideas in a new paragraph. Be sure your ideas are complete sentences. Change nouns, verbs, and adjectives to more specific words.

The next draft should show improvements in organization and detail of information when compared with the first draft.

Day #4

proofread

Proofread your new paragraph. Are any words misspelled? Did you use the correct verb form? Make sure your capitalization and punctuation are correct. Mark the corrections with proofreading marks.

- ❒ ✓ Capitalization Mistakes
- ❒ ✓ Odd Grammar
- ❒ ✓ Punctuation Mistakes
- ❒ ✓ Spelling Mistakes

The final draft should show proofreading marks where needed.

Published by Frank Schaffer Publications. Copyright protected. 23 0-7682-3225-2 *Write 4 Today*

Name **Week #6**

Assessment #6

publish

Now it is time to publish your writing. Write your final copy on the lines below.

MAKE SURE it turns out:

- NEAT—Make sure there are no wrinkles, creases, or holes.
- CLEAN—Erase any smudges or dirty spots.
- EASY TO READ—Use your best handwriting and good spacing between words.

The content of writing samples will vary. Check to be sure that students have correctly completed all of the earlier steps in the writing process and have followed instructions for publishing their work. Use rubric on page 5 to assess.

Published by Frank Schaffer Publications. Copyright protected. 24 0-7682-3225-2 *Write 4 Today*

Answer Key

Name **Week #7**

Underline with three short lines the first letter of words that need to be capitalized.
1. when i think of kentucky, i think of the kentucky derby.

Underline the complete subject and circle the simple subject in the sentence.
2. The best horse (race) in the world has many beautiful horses.

Use proofreading marks to correct the punctuation in the sentence.
3. When you think of Kentucky, what do you think of?

Circle the correct word in the sentence.
4. The (principle/(principal)) of my school visited Kentucky.

Day #1

Underline with three short lines the first letter of words that need to be capitalized.
1. when i think of indiana, i think of the indy 500.

Underline the complete subject and circle the simple subject in the sentence.
2. That famous car (race) is my dad's favorite sporting event.

Use proofreading marks to correct the punctuation in the sentence.
3. Massachusetts reminds me of the Boston Marathon, the Boston Red Sox, and the Boston Tea Party.

Circle the correct word in the sentence.
4. Do you want to go ((there)/their/they're)?

Day #2

Underline with three short lines the first letter of words that need to be capitalized.
1. i think of the dallas cowboys and the houston astros when i think of texas.

Underline the complete subject and circle the simple subject in the sentence.
2. The football (players) in Texas are strong.

Use proofreading marks to correct the punctuation in the sentence.
3. Some states have several sports teams, like football, baseball, and basketball.

Circle the correct word in the sentence.
4. I think football is (grate/(great))!

Day #3

Underline with three short lines the first letter of words that need to be capitalized.
1. rhode island and south dakota don't have professional football teams.

Underline the complete subject and circle the simple subject in the sentence.
2. (Sports) provide entertainment for millions of people.

Use proofreading marks to correct the punctuation in the sentence.
3. Millions of people watch competitions on television, listen to the games on the radio, or go to the games.

Circle the correct word in the sentence.
4. Do you have a favorite sports ((team)/teem)?

Day #4

Published by Frank Schaffer Publications. Copyright protected. 25 0-7682-3225-2 *Write 4 Today*

Name **Week #7**

Assessment

Assessment #7

Read the paragraph. Find the eight errors in the paragraph and correct them using proofreading marks.

Excited crowds in many states attend sporting events every week. Fans follow ~~there~~ their (sp) favorite ~~teems~~ teams (sp). What is your favorite sport? I like a lot of sports. I like to watch the Yankees, the red Sox, and the blue Jays when they play.

Now rewrite the paragraph correctly. In the first sentence, underline the complete subject and circle the simple subject.

Excited (crowds) in many states attend sporting events every week. Fans follow their favorite teams. What is your favorite sport? I like a lot of sports. I like to watch the Yankees, the Red Sox, and the Blue Jays when they play.

Published by Frank Schaffer Publications. Copyright protected. 26 0-7682-3225-2 *Write 4 Today*

Name **Week #8**

prewrite/brainstorm

To finish the multi-paragraph essay you worked on in week #4 and week #6, you must decide what to write in your conclusion paragraph. On a separate sheet of paper, draw a clustering map. Write your topic in the center circle. Then write your main ideas in other circles.

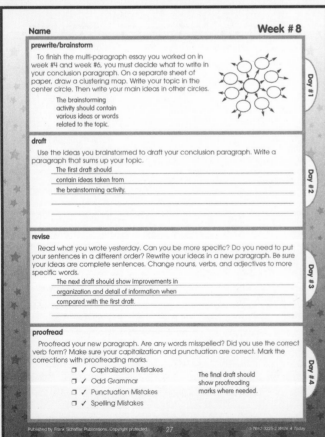

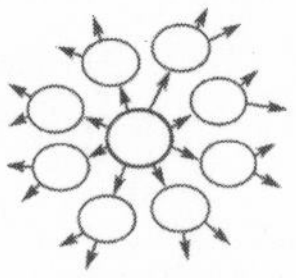

The brainstorming activity should contain various ideas or words related to the topic.

Day #1

draft

Use the ideas you brainstormed to draft your conclusion paragraph. Write a paragraph that sums up your topic.

The first draft should contain ideas taken from the brainstorming activity.

Day #2

revise

Read what you wrote yesterday. Can you be more specific? Do you need to put your sentences in a different order? Rewrite your ideas in a new paragraph. Be sure your ideas are complete sentences. Change nouns, verbs, and adjectives to more specific words.

The next draft should show improvements in organization and detail of information when compared with the first draft.

Day #3

proofread

Proofread your new paragraph. Are any words misspelled? Did you use the correct verb form? Make sure your capitalization and punctuation are correct. Mark the corrections with proofreading marks.

- ❒ ✓ Capitalization Mistakes
- ❒ ✓ Odd Grammar
- ❒ ✓ Punctuation Mistakes
- ❒ ✓ Spelling Mistakes

The final draft should show proofreading marks where needed.

Day #4

Published by Frank Schaffer Publications. Copyright protected. 27 0-7682-3225-2 *Write 4 Today*

Name **Week #8**

Assessment

Assessment #8

publish

Now it is time to publish your writing. Write your final copy on the lines below.
MAKE SURE it turns out:
- NEAT—Make sure there are no wrinkles, creases, or holes.
- CLEAN—Erase any smudges or dirty spots.
- EASY TO READ—Use your best handwriting and good spacing between words.

The content of writing samples will vary. Check to be sure that students have correctly completed all of the earlier steps in the writing process and have followed instructions for publishing their work. Use rubric on page 5 to assess.

Published by Frank Schaffer Publications. Copyright protected. 28 0-7682-3225-2 *Write 4 Today*

Answer Key

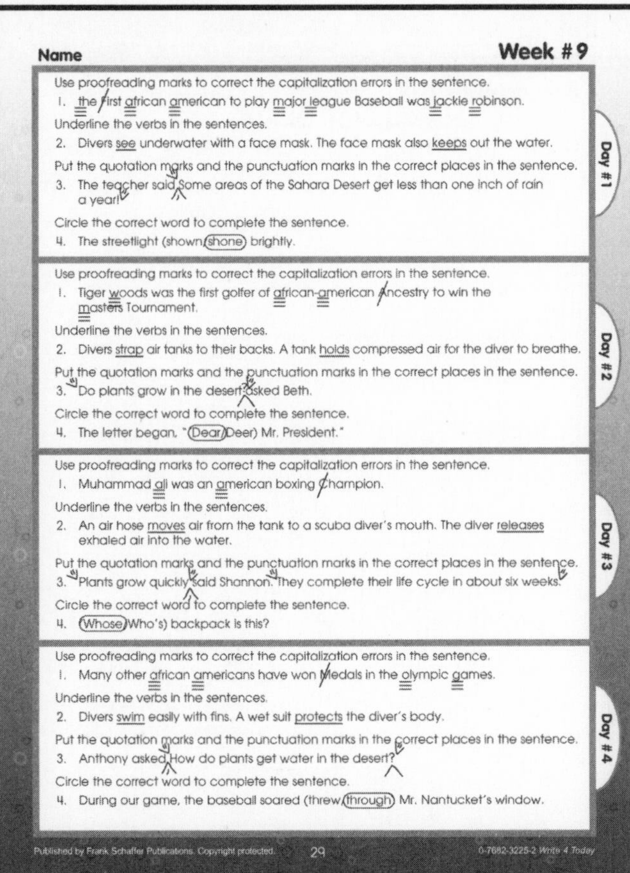

Name **Week #9**

Use proofreading marks to correct the capitalization errors in the sentence.
1. the first african american to play major league Baseball was jackie robinson.

Underline the verbs in the sentences.
2. Divers see underwater with a face mask. The face mask also keeps out the water.

Put the quotation marks and the punctuation marks in the correct places in the sentence.
3. The teacher said, "Some areas of the Sahara Desert get less than one inch of rain a year."

Circle the correct word to complete the sentence.
4. The streetlight (shown/shone) brightly.

Day #1

Use proofreading marks to correct the capitalization errors in the sentence.
1. Tiger woods was the first golfer of african-american Ancestry to win the masters Tournament.

Underline the verbs in the sentences.
2. Divers strap air tanks to their backs. A tank holds compressed air for the diver to breathe.

Put the quotation marks and the punctuation marks in the correct places in the sentence.
3. "Do plants grow in the desert?" asked Beth.

Circle the correct word to complete the sentence.
4. The letter began, "(Dear/Deer) Mr. President."

Day #2

Use proofreading marks to correct the capitalization errors in the sentence.
1. Muhammad ali was an american boxing Champion.

Underline the verbs in the sentences.
2. An air hose moves air from the tank to a scuba diver's mouth. The diver releases exhaled air into the water.

Put the quotation marks and the punctuation marks in the correct places in the sentence.
3. "Plants grow quickly," said Shannon. "They complete their life cycle in about six weeks."

Circle the correct word to complete the sentence.
4. (Whose/Who's) backpack is this?

Day #3

Use proofreading marks to correct the capitalization errors in the sentence.
1. Many other african americans have won Medals in the olympic games.

Underline the verbs in the sentences.
2. Divers swim easily with fins. A wet suit protects the diver's body.

Put the quotation marks and the punctuation marks in the correct places in the sentence.
3. Anthony asked, "How do plants get water in the desert?"

Circle the correct word to complete the sentence.
4. During our game, the baseball soared (threw/through) Mr. Nantucket's window.

Day #4

Published by Frank Schaffer Publications. Copyright protected. 29 0-7682-3225-2 *Write 4 Today*

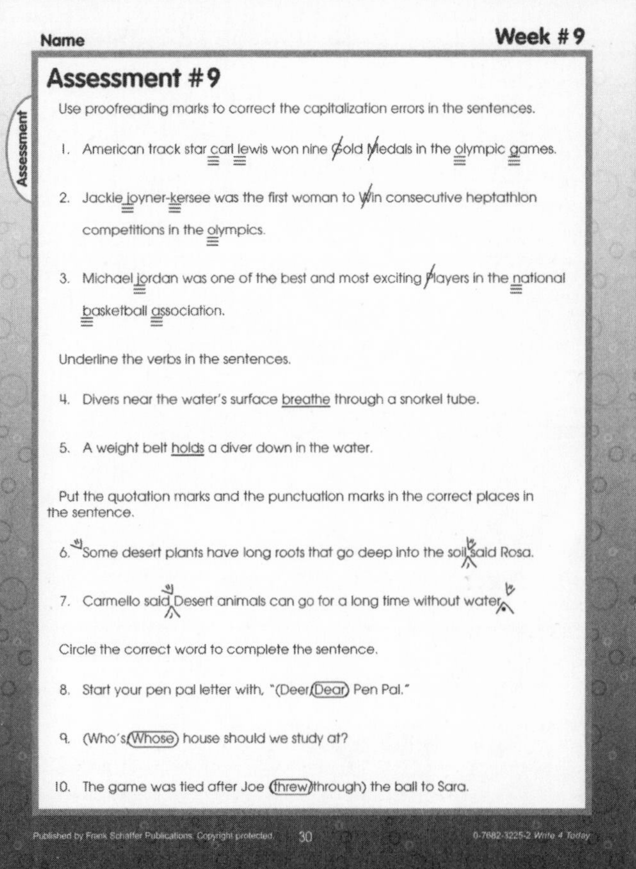

Name **Week #9**

Assessment #9

Assessment

Use proofreading marks to correct the capitalization errors in the sentences.

1. American track star carl lewis won nine Gold Medals in the olympic games.
2. Jackie joyner-kersee was the first woman to Win consecutive heptathlon competitions in the olympics.
3. Michael jordan was one of the best and most exciting Players in the national basketball association.

Underline the verbs in the sentences.

4. Divers near the water's surface breathe through a snorkel tube.
5. A weight belt holds a diver down in the water.

Put the quotation marks and the punctuation marks in the correct places in the sentence.

6. "Some desert plants have long roots that go deep into the soil," said Rosa.
7. Carmello said, "Desert animals can go for a long time without water."

Circle the correct word to complete the sentence.

8. Start your pen pal letter with, "(Deer/Dear) Pen Pal."
9. (Who's/Whose) house should we study at?
10. The game was tied after Joe (threw/through) the ball to Sara.

Published by Frank Schaffer Publications. Copyright protected. 30 0-7682-3225-2 *Write 4 Today*

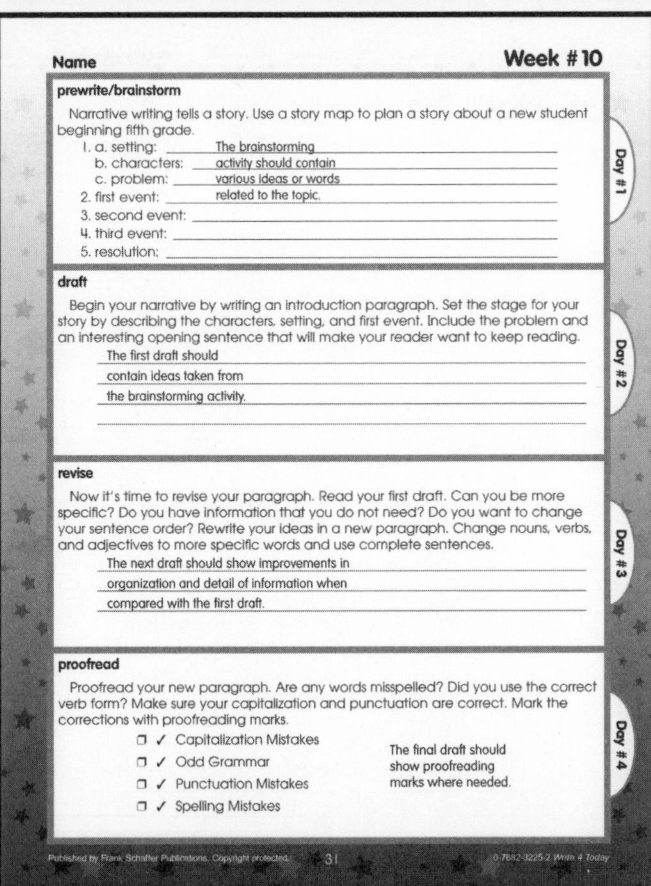

Name **Week #10**

prewrite/brainstorm

Narrative writing tells a story. Use a story map to plan a story about a new student beginning fifth grade.

1. a. setting: The brainstorming
   b. characters: activity should contain
   c. problem: various ideas or words
2. first event: related to the topic.
3. second event:
4. third event:
5. resolution:

Day #1

draft

Begin your narrative by writing an introduction paragraph. Set the stage for your story by describing the characters, setting, and first event. Include the problem and an interesting opening sentence that will make your reader want to keep reading.

The first draft should contain ideas taken from the brainstorming activity.

Day #2

revise

Now it's time to revise your paragraph. Read your first draft. Can you be more specific? Do you have information that you do not need? Do you want to change your sentence order? Rewrite your ideas in a new paragraph. Change nouns, verbs, and adjectives to more specific words and use complete sentences.

The next draft should show improvements in organization and detail of information when compared with the first draft.

Day #3

proofread

Proofread your new paragraph. Are any words misspelled? Did you use the correct verb form? Make sure your capitalization and punctuation are correct. Mark the corrections with proofreading marks.

- ❐ ✓ Capitalization Mistakes
- ❐ ✓ Odd Grammar
- ❐ ✓ Punctuation Mistakes
- ❐ ✓ Spelling Mistakes

The final draft should show proofreading marks where needed.

Day #4

Published by Frank Schaffer Publications. Copyright protected. 31 0-7682-3225-2 *Write 4 Today*

Name **Week #10**

Assessment #10

Assessment

publish

Now it is time to publish your writing. Write your final copy on the lines below.

MAKE SURE it turns out:

- NEAT—Make sure there are no wrinkles, creases, or holes.
- CLEAN—Erase any smudges or dirty spots.
- EASY TO READ—Use your best handwriting and good spacing between words.

The content of writing samples will vary. Check to be sure that students have correctly completed all of the earlier steps in the writing process and have followed instructions for publishing their work. Use rubric on page 5 to assess.

Published by Frank Schaffer Publications. Copyright protected. 32 0-7682-3225-2 *Write 4 Today*

Answer Key

Name **Week # 11**

Day #1

Circle the choice that shows the right capitalization.
1. a. *Harry Potter And The Order Of The Phoenix*
   ⓑ *Harry Potter and the Order of the Phoenix*
   c. *Harry Potter and The Order of The Phoenix*

Circle the choice that shows the right spelling.
2. ________ is wrong here.
   a. Sumthing
   b. Some thing
   ⓒ Something
   d. Sum Thing

Read the pair of sentences. Rewrite the pair correctly.
3. She don't get it. Yes, she do! She doesn't get it. Yes, she does!

Commas separate words in a series of three or more. Colons introduce a list. Using proofreading marks, add the missing punctuation to the sentence.
4. Pack these things in a backpack for the bus trip: a snack, a water bottle, sunscreen, and a hat.

Day #2

Circle the choice that shows the right capitalization.
1. a. *My Dog is from Pluto*
   b. *My dog Is from pluto*
   ⓒ *My Dog Is from Pluto*

Circle the choice that shows the right spelling.
2. My ________ music is jazz.
   a. favrite
   b. faverite
   c. favarite
   ⓓ favorite

Read the pair of sentences. Rewrite the pair correctly.
3. He don't like it. Yes, he do! He doesn't like it. Yes, he does!

Commas separate words in a series of three or more. Colons introduce a list. Using proofreading marks, add the missing punctuation to the sentence.
4. Do not bring these items to Camp Porcupine: gum, candy, money, and electronic gadgets.

Day #3

Circle the choice that shows the right capitalization.
1. ⓐ *Tuck Everlasting*
   b. *Tuck EverLasting*
   c. *Tuck everlasting*

Circle the choice that shows the right spelling.
2. We ________ finished the test.
   a. finely
   b. finelly
   ⓒ finally
   d. finaly

[illegible] the pair of sentences. Rewrite the pair correctly.
3. [illegible] don't matter. Yes, it do! It doesn't matter. Yes, it does!

C[illegible] separate words in a series of three or more. Colons introduce a list. Using proofreading ma[illegible] the missing punctuation to the sentence.
4. [illegible]rs, counselors, and activity leaders are assigned to units at Camp Porcupine.

Day #4

Circle the [illegible] that shows the right capitalization.
1. a. *Har[illegible]e Spy*
   ⓑ *Harr[illegible] Spy*
   c. *Harri[illegible]spy*

Circle the choice that shows the right spelling.
2. ________ house is white with a blue roof.
   a. Or
   b. Hour
   c. Oure
   ⓓ Our

Read the pair of [illegible]nces. Rewrite the pair correctly.
2. My mom don['t wan]t me to learn this. Yes, she do! My mom doesn't want me to learn this. Yes, she does!

Commas separate [illegible] in a series of three or more. Colons introduce a list. Using proofreading marks, add the missi[ng pu]nctuation to the sentence.
3. Each unit has thes[e str]uctures: six camper tents, two staff tents, two bathrooms, and one shower house.

Published by Frank Schaffer P[illegible]s. Copyright protected. 33 0-7682-3225-2 *Write 4 Today*

Name **Week # 11**

Assessment # 11

Circle the choice that shows the right capitalization.
1. a. *Island of The Blue Dolphins*
   b. *Island Of The Blue Dolphins*
   ⓒ *Island of the Blue Dolphins*

2. a. *The Westing game*
   ⓑ *The Westing Game*
   c. *the Westing Game*

Read the pairs of sentences. Rewrite each pair correctly.
3. My dad don't notice if I speak incorrectly. Yes, he do!
   My dad doesn't notice if I speak incorrectly.
   Yes, he does!
4. My family don't care about school. Yes, it do!
   My family doesn't care about school.
   Yes, it does!

Commas separate words in a series of three or more. Colons introduce a list. Using proofreading marks, add the missing punctuation to the sentence.
5. Eagle, Coyote, and Grizzly Bear are the three girls' units.
6. The boys' units are Fox, Hawk, and Elk.
7. You must do these lodge chores when your unit has meal duty: set the tables, serve food, clear the dishes, clean the tables, and sweep the floors.

Rewrite these words correctly on the lines.
8. sumthing something
9. faverit favorite
10. finaly finally

Published by Frank Schaffer Publications. Copyright protected. 34 0-7682-3225-2 *Write 4 Today*

Name **Week # 12**

Day #1

prewrite/brainstorm

Continue writing the narrative you started on week 10. Look back at the first two events on your story map. Make a list of descriptive words about the second event.

second event:

The brainstorming activity should contain various ideas or words related to the topic.

Day #2

draft

Now draft a paragraph describing the second event that happened when a new student began fifth grade. Use the ideas you wrote on your brainstorming list.

The first draft should contain ideas taken from the brainstorming activity.

Day #3

revise

Now it's time to revise your paragraphs about the new student. Read your first draft. Can you be more specific? Do you have information that you do not need? Do you want to change your sentence order? Rewrite your paragraph. Change nouns, verbs, and adjectives to more specific words and use complete sentences.

The next draft should show improvements in organization and detail of information when compared with the first draft.

Day #4

proofread

Proofread your paragraph about the new student. Are any words misspelled? Did you use the correct verb form? Make sure your capitalization and punctuation are correct. Mark the corrections with proofreading marks.

- ❒ ✓ Capitalization Mistakes
- ❒ ✓ Odd Grammar
- ❒ ✓ Punctuation Mistakes
- ❒ ✓ Spelling Mistakes

The final draft should show proofreading marks where needed.

Published by Frank Schaffer Publications. Copyright protected. 35 0-7682-3225-2 *Write 4 Today*

Name **Week # 12**

Assessment # 12

publish

Now it is time to publish your writing. Write your final copy on the lines below. MAKE SURE it turns out:

- NEAT—Make sure there are no wrinkles, creases, or holes.
- CLEAN—Erase any smudges or dirty spots.
- EASY TO READ—Use your best handwriting and good spacing between words.

The content of writing samples will vary. Check to be sure that students have correctly completed all of the earlier steps in the writing process and have followed instructions for publishing their work. Use rubic on page 5 to assess.

Published by Frank Schaffer Publications. Copyright protected. 36 0-7682-3225-2 *Write 4 Today*

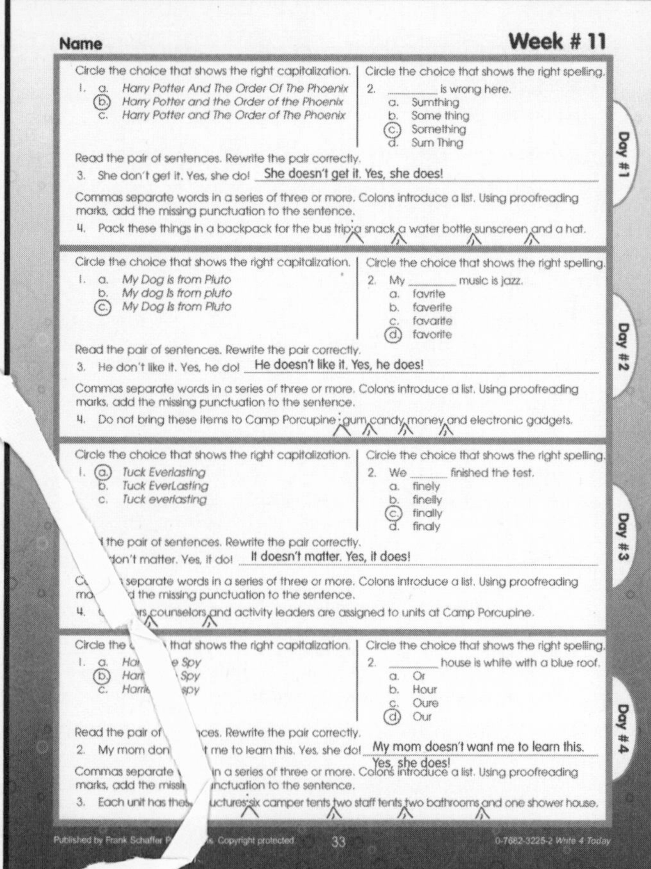

Answer Key

Name **Week #13**

Day #1

Underline with three short lines the first letter of words that need to be capitalized.

1. did the movie *around the world in 80 days* win an academy award in 1956?

Draw a line under the complete predicate. Circle the predicate verb.

2. Joan and I cheered for our favorite team.

Add quotation marks, underlining, and punctuation where necessary in the sentence.

3. The Olympic Games were held in Stockholm Sweden in 1912 replied vivian

Homonyms are words that sound alike but have different meanings and spellings. Circle the correct words in the sentence.

4. My library book was (dew/due) last (week/weak).

Day #2

Underline with three short lines the first letter of words that need to be capitalized.

1. robert burns, the poet, wrote "auld lang syne."

Draw a line under the complete predicate. Circle the predicate verb.

2. Chris dropped one more quarter into the machine.

Add quotation marks, underlining, and punctuation where necessary in the sentence.

3. Monica yelled Wow did you see that car?

Circle the correct words in the sentence.

4. Did those (ate/eight) (flowers/flours) come from your yard?

Day #3

Underline with three short lines the first letter of words that need to be capitalized.

1. does grandpa get the *chicago sun times* or the *chicago tribune*?

Draw a line under the complete predicate. Circle the predicate verb.

2. The clerk examined the jacket carefully.

Add quotation marks, underlining, and punctuation where necessary in the sentence.

3. Look out screamed Andy

Circle the correct words in the sentence.

4. Frances (scent/sent) her (aunt/ant) a birthday card.

Day #4

Underline with three short lines the first letter of words that need to be capitalized.

1. we're going to an italian restaurant on friday night after we read *strega nona.*

Draw a line under the complete predicate. Circle the predicate verb.

2. Margie's dog, Bandit, is a frisky animal.

Add quotation marks, underlining, and punctuation, where necessary in the sentence.

3. Bobby our class president took charge of today's meeting

Circle the correct words in the sentence.

4. (Too/To/Two) dollars is a (fare/fair) price.

Published by Frank Schaffer Publications. Copyright protected. 37 0-7682-3225-2 *Write 4 Today*

Name **Week #13**

Assessment

Assessment #13

Using proofreading marks, mark the first letter of words that need to be capitalized and add punctuation to the sentences.

1. i received the book *the life cycle book of cats* from grandmother

2. will judge j.t. otis preside today?

3. dad, *the los angeles times* was not delivered this morning said doug

4. dorians deli carries turkish candy remarked peggy

Draw a line under the complete predicate in the sentences. Circle the predicate verb.

5. My teacher asked for volunteers.
6. The birds ate all the seeds.
7. Rex and I are in the same race.

Circle the correct words in the sentences.

8. Dad (sent/scent) Mom (flower/flours) for her birthday.
9. We have (too/two) more (weeks/weaks) until this is (due/dew).
10. Can you imagine having (eight/ate) uncles and (ants/aunts)?

Published by Frank Schaffer Publications. Copyright protected. 38 0-7682-3225-2 *Write 4 Today*

Name **Week #14**

Day #1

prewrite/brainstorm

It is time to write about the third event in the narrative you worked on in weeks 10 and 12. Look back at what you wrote for that event on your story map. Take that idea and make a list of descriptive words about the third event.

third event:

The brainstorming activity should contain various ideas or words related to the topic.

Day #2

draft

Conclude your narrative by drafting a paragraph that wraps up everything that happened when a new student began fifth grade. Use the ideas you wrote on your brainstorming list. Be sure to include the resolution to the story problem.

The first draft should contain ideas taken from the brainstorming activity.

Day #3

revise

Now it's time to revise your paragraphs about the new student. Read your first draft. Can you be more specific? Do you have information that you do not need? Do you want to change your sentence order? Rewrite your paragraph. Change nouns, verbs, and adjectives to more specific words and use complete sentences.

The next draft should show improvements in organization and detail of information when compared with the first draft.

Day #4

proofread

Proofread your paragraph about the new student. Are any words misspelled? Did you use the correct verb form? Make sure your capitalization and punctuation are correct. Mark the corrections with proofreading marks.

- ❒ ✓ Capitalization Mistakes
- ❒ ✓ Odd Grammar
- ❒ ✓ Punctuation Mistakes
- ❒ ✓ Spelling Mistakes

The final draft should show proofreading marks where needed.

Published by Frank Schaffer Publications. Copyright protected. 39 0-7682-3225-2 *Write 4 Today*

Name **Week #14**

Assessment

Assessment #14

publish

Now it is time to publish your writing. Write your final copy on the lines below.

MAKE SURE it turns out:

- NEAT—Make sure there are no wrinkles, creases, or holes.
- CLEAN—Erase any smudges or dirty spots.
- EASY TO READ—Use your best handwriting and good spacing between words.

The content of writing samples will vary. Check to be sure that students have correctly completed all of the earlier steps in the writing process and have followed instructions for publishing their work. Use rubic on page 5 to assess.

Published by Frank Schaffer Publications. Copyright protected. 40 0-7682-3225-2 *Write 4 Today*

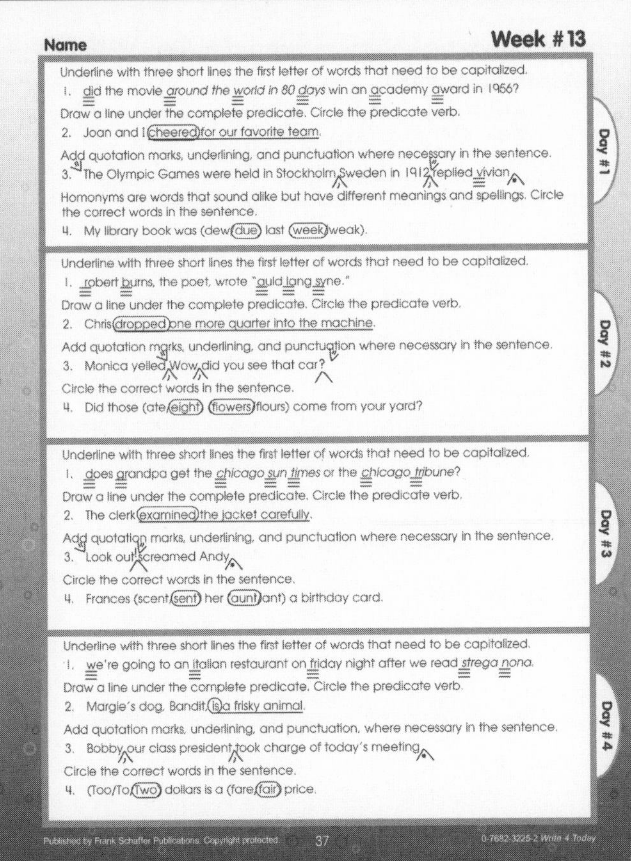

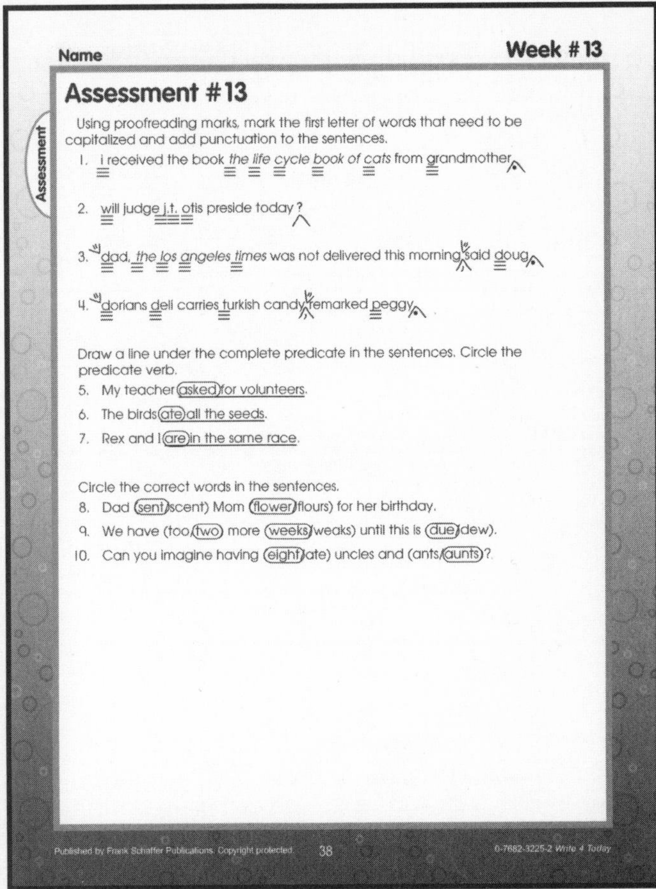

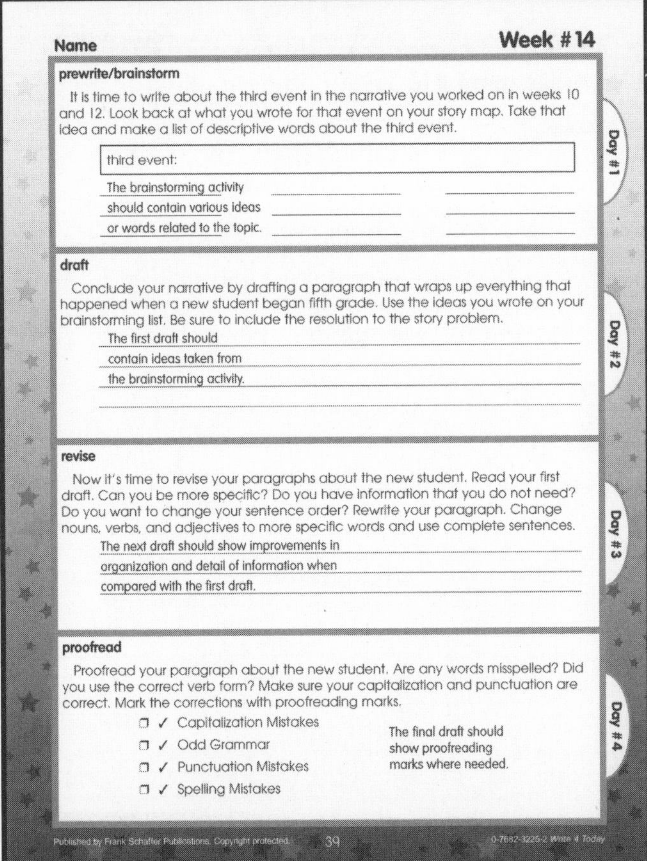

Answer Key

Name **Week #15**

Day #1

Use proofreading marks to correct the capitalization errors in the sentence.

1. Last Winter, the students voted to have Music played in the Cafeteria during lunch on fridays.

Fill in the circle next to the correct interrogative pronoun.

2. ________ should I call in case of an emergency?
   ○ Who ● Whom

Complete the sentence so it contains a direct quotation. Add quotation marks, commas, and end punctuation.

3. Ellen shouted, Answers will vary.

Use proofreading marks to correct the words that are not spelled correctly.

4. Have you ever wanted to ~~shair~~ share (sp) a secret with someone without anyone else ~~nowing~~ knowing (sp)?

Day #2

Use proofreading marks to correct the capitalization errors in the sentence.

1. soon after the students voted, the question was asked, "what kind of Music do students want?"

Fill in the circle next to the correct interrogative pronoun.

2. ________ left the dirty dishes in the sink?
   ● Who ○ Whom

Complete the sentence so it contains a direct quotation. Add quotation marks, commas, and end punctuation.

3. Jackie said, Answers will vary.

Use proofreading marks to correct the words that are not spelled correctly.

4. ~~Heare~~ Here's (sp) a way you can write a secret ~~mesage~~ message (sp). It's ~~easey~~ easy (sp) and fun to do!

Day #3

Use proofreading marks to correct the capitalization errors in the sentence.

1. The Principal let Students put classical, Oldies, Country, and rock on the ballot.

Fill in the circle next to the correct interrogative pronoun.

2. ________ called?
   ● Who ○ Whom

Complete the sentence so it contains a direct quotation. Add quotation marks, commas, and end punctuation.

3. The children shouted, Answers will vary.

Use proofreading marks to correct the words that are not spelled correctly.

4. You ~~shuld~~ should (sp) start ~~bye~~ by (sp) squeezing the ~~jooce~~ juice (sp) from a lemon into a small ~~bole~~ bowl (sp).

Day #4

Use proofreading marks to correct the capitalization errors in the sentence.

1. Principal pecoraro said she would respect the Students' choice.

Fill in the circle next to the correct interrogative pronoun.

2. ________ do you think we should invite to the party?
   ○ Who ● Whom

Complete the sentence so it contains a direct quotation. Add quotation marks, commas, and end punctuation.

3. The teacher asked, Answers will vary.

Use proofreading marks to correct the words that are not spelled correctly.

4. Use a toothpick ~~two~~ to (sp) write your secret message with lemon ~~jooce~~ juice (sp). Let it ~~drie~~ dry (sp).

Published by Frank Schaffer Publications. Copyright protected. 41 0-7682-3225-2 *Write 4 Today*

Name **Week #15**

Assessment #15

Use proofreading marks to correct the capitalization errors in the sentences.

1. Principal pecoraro said that she had her own Music likes and dislikes.
2. The Students voted to let the teachers and the Principal vote, too.
3. you can hear the results of the Vote every friday at lunch!

Fill in the circle next to the correct interrogative pronoun.

4. _____ took my sunglasses?
   ● Who ○ Whom
5. _____ is responsible for this mess?
   ● Who ○ Whom
6. To _____ did you give the prize?
   ○ who ● whom

Complete the sentence so it contains a direct quotation. Add quotation marks, commas, and end punctuation.

7. Patty exclaimed, "Answers will vary."
8. "Will you," Linda asked, "Answers will vary."

Use proofreading marks to correct the words that are not spelled correctly.

9. Ask an adult ~~too~~ to (sp) put the paper in an oven. The oven ~~shuld~~ should (sp) be heated to 350 degrees for eight to ten minutes.
10. The heat will react with the lemon ~~joice~~ juice (sp). This will make your ~~mesage~~ message (sp) appear!

Published by Frank Schaffer Publications. Copyright protected. 42 0-7682-3225-2 *Write 4 Today*

Name **Week #16**

Day #1

prewrite/brainstorm

A biography is the story of a person's life. Think of someone you know and would like to write a biography about. It could be someone in your family, a friend, or a neighbor. On a separate sheet of paper, write down the answers to the questions on the right.

The brainstorming activity should contain various ideas or words related to the topic.

1. Where and when was this person born?
2. What were the family and home of this person like?
3. Where did this person go to school?
4. What jobs has this person had?
5. What special interests, hobbies, sports, or crafts does this person enjoy?
6. What interesting things have happened to this person?

Day #2

draft

Continue working on the biography. Look at the answers you wrote for the six questions. Now, draft a paragraph about that person using the information. Include a topic sentence and a conclusion.

The first draft should contain ideas taken from the brainstorming activity.

Day #3

revise

Read what you wrote yesterday. Can you be more specific? Do you have information that does not support your topic sentence? Do you need to change your sentence order? Rewrite your ideas in a new paragraph. Change nouns, verbs, and adjectives to more specific words.

The next draft should show improvements in organization and detail of information when compared with the first draft.

Day #4

proofread

Proofread your new paragraph. Are any words misspelled? Did you use the correct verb form? Make sure your capitalization and punctuation are correct. Mark the corrections with proofreading marks.

- ❒ ✓ Capitalization Mistakes
- ❒ ✓ Odd Grammar
- ❒ ✓ Punctuation Mistakes
- ❒ ✓ Spelling Mistakes

The final draft should show proofreading marks where needed.

Published by Frank Schaffer Publications. Copyright protected. 43 0-7682-3225-2 *Write 4 Today*

Name **Week #16**

Assessment #16

publish

Now it is time to publish your writing. Write your final copy on the lines below. MAKE SURE it turns out:

- NEAT—Make sure there are no wrinkles, creases, or holes.
- CLEAN—Erase any smudges or dirty spots.
- EASY TO READ—Use your best handwriting and good spacing between words.

The content of writing samples will vary. Check to be sure that students have correctly completed all of the earlier steps in the writing process and have followed instructions for publishing their work. Use rubic on page 5 to assess.

Published by Frank Schaffer Publications. Copyright protected. 44 0-7682-3225-2 *Write 4 Today*

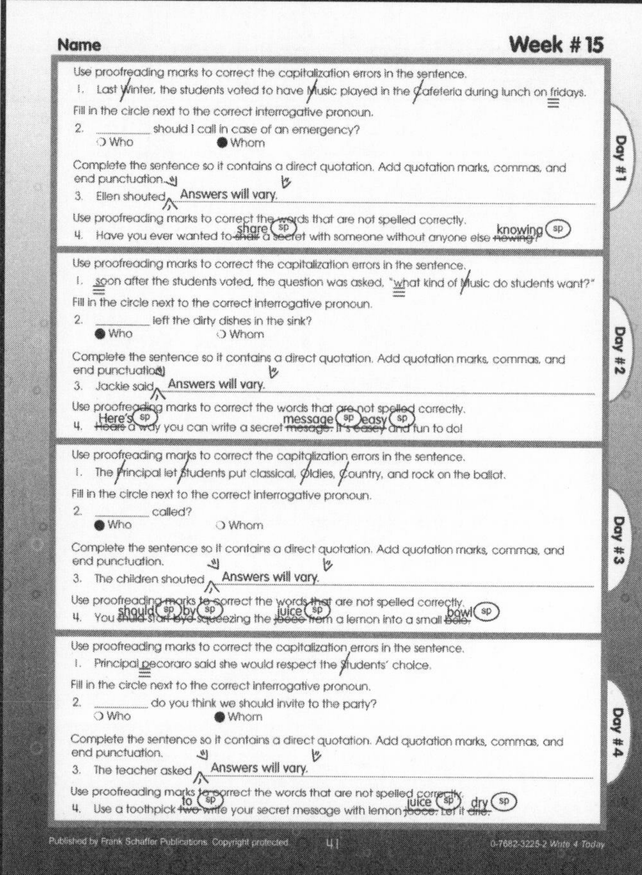

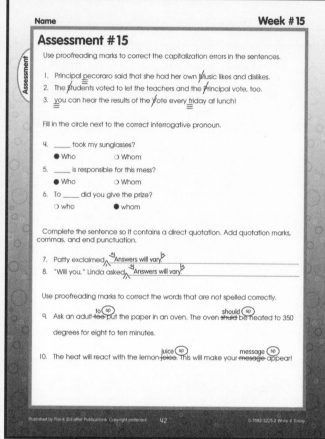

Answer Key

Name **Week #17**

Day #1

Circle the choice that shows the right capitalization.

1. a. tuesday, january 22
   b. tuesday, January 22
   (c.) Tuesday, January 22

Circle the correct word.

2. (He, Him) and Brenda are (hour, our) cousins.

Mark the sentence to add the missing punctuation.

3. Kathy and Leopold entered the capsule.

Circle the correct word for the sentence.

4. My dad (lies, lays) in the hammock for hours.

Day #2

Circle the choice that shows the right capitalization.

1. a. Our teacher is mr. Coviak.
   b. Our Teacher is Mr. Coviak.
   (c.) Our teacher is Mr. Coviak.

Circle the correct word.

2. (Affects, Effects) of the earthquake can be seen everywhere (accept, except) the shelter.

Mark the sentence to add the missing punctuation.

3. What is their mission?

Circle the correct word for the sentence.

4. Mike has (lain, laid) his scissors on the desk.

Day #3

Circle the choice that shows the right capitalization.

1. a. *The house on the hill*
   (b.) *The House on the Hill*
   c. *The House On the Hill*

Circle the correct word.

2. Every one of the (us, we) boys passed (their, his) test.

Mark the sentence to add the missing punctuation.

3. Look out! It's an asteroid!

Circle the correct word for the sentence.

4. The papers have (laid, lain) on the desk for weeks.

Day #4

Circle the choice that shows the right capitalization.

1. (a.) Police Chief Harry Martinez
   b. Police Chief Harry martinez
   c. Police chief Harry Martinez

Circle the correct word.

2. Dorene and (I, me) helped Wanda with (she, her) homework.

Mark the sentence to add the missing punctuation.

3. Kathy calls back to the ship.

Circle the correct word for the sentence.

4. (Lay, Lie) down, Spot!

Published by Frank Schaffer Publications. Copyright protected. 45 0-7682-3225-2 *Write 4 Today*

Name **Week #17**

Assessment #17

Circle the choices that show the right capitalization.

1. a. *Fire marshall Penny Young*
   (b.) *Fire Marshall Penny Young*
   c. *fire marshall Penny Young*

2. a. *My Dog is from Pluto*
   b. *My dog Is from pluto*
   (c.) *My Dog Is from Pluto*

3. a. *Is Mr. Brown your Teacher?*
   b. *Is mr. Brown your teacher?*
   (c.) *Is Mr. Brown your teacher?*

Circle the correct word.

4. Richard and (she, her) did well in every subject (accept, except) history.
5. Uncle Bill thanked (us, we) children for (hour, our) concern.

Mark the sentences to add the missing punctuation.

6. They are on their way into deep space. or !
7. Before the launch, they checked their seat belts.
8. How long will it take them to get to the moon?

Circle the correct word for the sentence.

9. The lion (lies, lays) quietly, waiting for its prey.
10. You can (lie, lay) your coat on the chair.

Published by Frank Schaffer Publications. Copyright protected. 46 0-7682-3225-2 *Write 4 Today*

Name **Week #18**

Day #1

prewrite/brainstorm

In order to do anything—make a cake or give your dog a bath—you have to carry out a number of steps in the right order, or sequence. How do you make your favorite sandwich? For prewriting, make a list of the steps you take when you build your favorite sandwich.

The brainstorming activity should contain various ideas or words related to the topic.

Day #2

draft

Write a paragraph about how to make your favorite sandwich. Use words like *first, next, then,* and *finally* to help show the right order.

The first draft should contain ideas taken from the brainstorming activity.

Day #3

revise

Look at your draft. Did you begin with a sentence explaining what the paragraph is about? Did you put the sequence in the right order? Did you use words like *first, next, then,* and *finally* to help show the right order?

The next draft should show improvements in organization and detail of information when compared with the first draft.

Day #4

proofread

Proofread your new paragraph. Are any words misspelled? Did you use the correct verb form? Make sure your capitalization and punctuation are correct. Mark the corrections with proofreading marks.

- ❒ ✓ Capitalization Mistakes
- ❒ ✓ Odd Grammar
- ❒ ✓ Punctuation Mistakes
- ❒ ✓ Spelling Mistakes

The final draft should show proofreading marks where needed.

Published by Frank Schaffer Publications. Copyright protected. 47 0-7682-3225-2 *Write 4 Today*

Name **Week #18**

Assessment #18

publish

Now it is time to publish your writing. Write your final copy on the lines below.

MAKE SURE it turns out:

- NEAT—Make sure there are no wrinkles, creases, or holes.
- CLEAN—Erase any smudges or dirty spots.
- EASY TO READ—Use your best handwriting and good spacing between words.

The content of writing samples will vary. Check to be sure that students have correctly completed all of the earlier steps in the writing process and have followed instructions for publishing their work. Use rubic on page 5 to assess.

Published by Frank Schaffer Publications. Copyright protected. 48 0-7682-3225-2 *Write 4 Today*

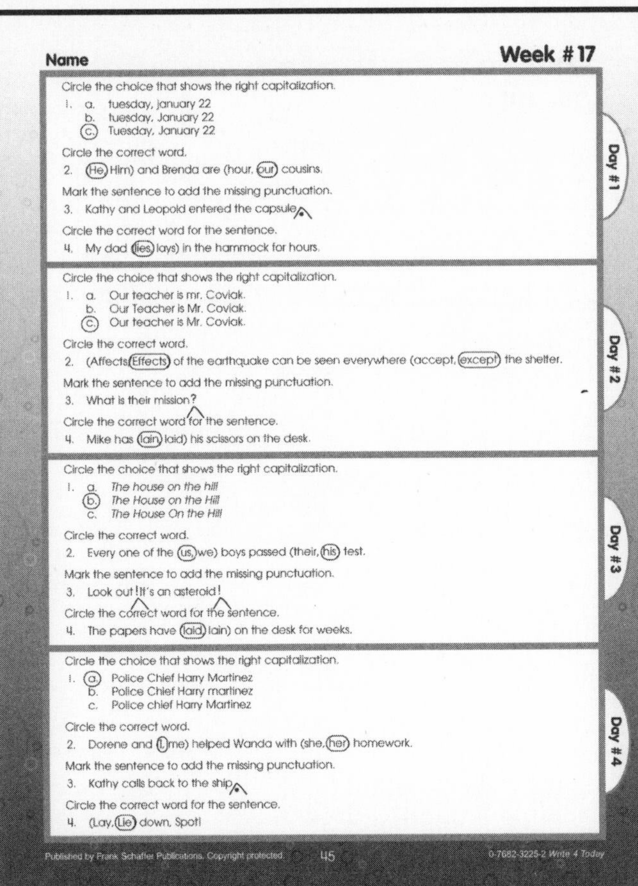

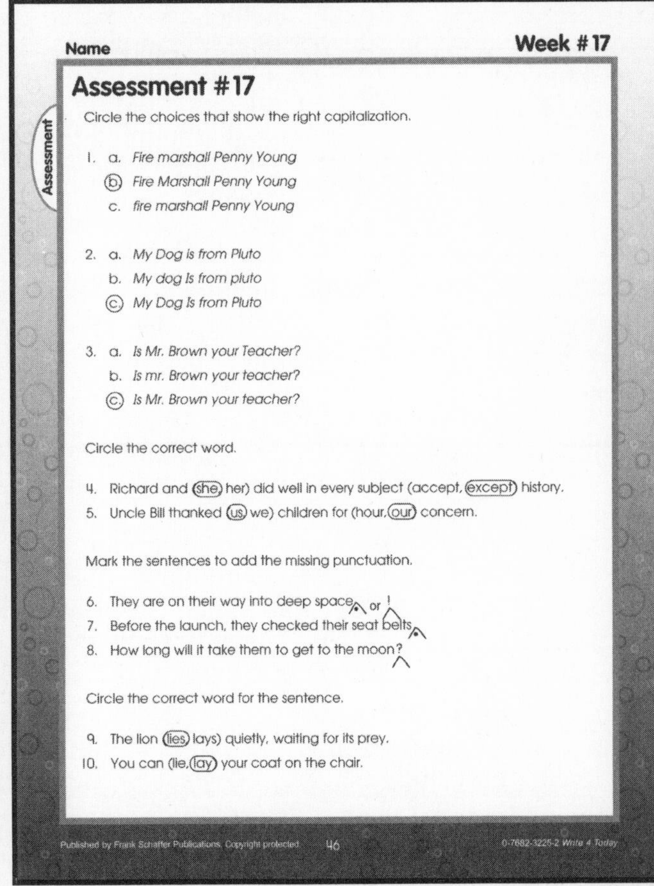

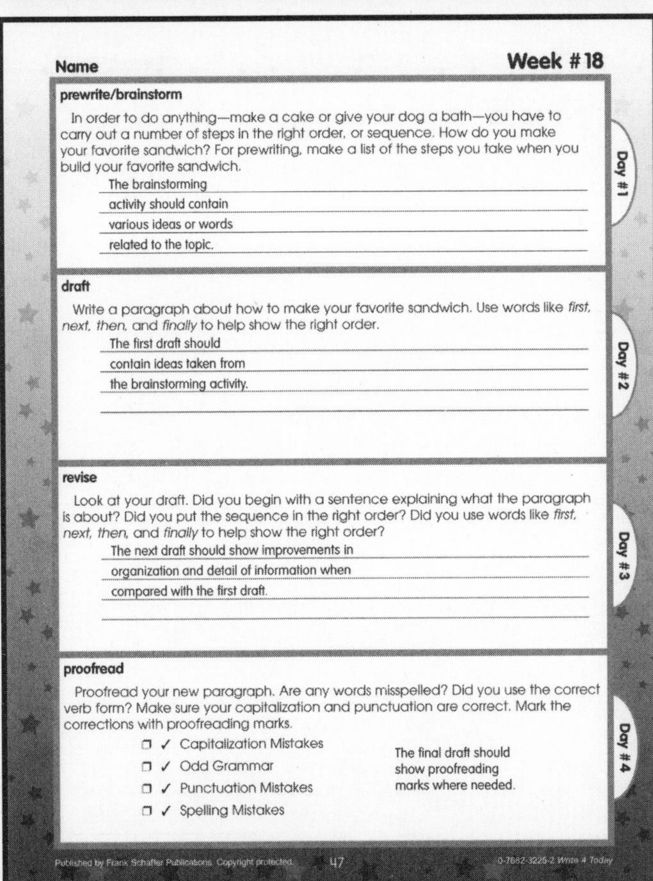

Answer Key

Name **Week #19**

Underline with three short lines the first letter of words that need to be capitalized.

1. last may i wrote a poem called "oodles of noodles."

Draw a line under the complete subject. Circle the simple subject.

2. The tired kitten curled up in front of the warm fireplace.

Add quotation marks and other punctuation where necessary in the sentence.

3. The title of my new poem is By the Seaside

Homonyms are words that sound alike but have different meanings and spellings. Circle the correct words in the sentence.

4. When did Lena (sow so sew) that (knew new) dress?

Day #1

Underline with three short lines the first letter of words that need to be capitalized.

1. when we flew to texas, terry read the entire *skater's world* magazine.

Draw a line under the complete subject. Circle the simple subject.

2. Nancy washed the dishes after lunch.

Add quotation marks and other punctuation where necessary in the sentence.

3. Does your brother still receive *Sesame Street Magazine*?

Circle the correct words in the sentence.

4. Karen went to (see sea) the (principal principle).

Day #2

Underline with three short lines the first letter of words that need to be capitalized.

1. gilbert and i read a book called *east of willow creek*.

Draw a line under the complete subject. Circle the simple subject.

2. That tall boy might become a good basketball player.

Add quotation marks and other punctuation where necessary in the sentence.

3. Our Battle of the Books team won said Lisa because we all read *Holes* and *Maniac Magee*.

Circle the correct words in the sentence.

4. Use good (stationary stationery) to (right write rite) your letter.

Day #3

Underline with three short lines the first letter of words that need to be capitalized.

1. joseph wrote for the rutgers university newspaper *the daily targum*.

Draw a line under the complete subject. Circle the simple subject.

2. The billowing black smoke could be seen for miles.

Add quotation marks and other punctuation where necessary in the sentence.

3. Keesha your dogs collar needs to be replaced

Circle the correct words in the sentence.

4. Yolanda drew a (strait straight) line across that (piece peace) of (would wood).

Day #4

Published by Frank Schaffer Publications. Copyright protected. 49 0-7682-3225-2 *Write 4 Today*

Name **Week #19**

Assessment

Assessment #19

Using proofreading marks, mark the first letter of words that need to be capitalized and add punctuation to the sentences.

1. i read the book *little women* in the fifth grade
2. maria wrote a poem called my favorite friend and i
3. dad, do you like the magazine *sports illustrated*?
4. grandmas favorite magazine is *family circle*

Draw a line under the complete subject. Circle the simple subject.

5. Pretty pink streamers hung from the ceiling.
6. The cool night air felt good after a long, hot day.
7. The large spider plant hung over the patio entrance.

Circle the correct words in the sentences.

8. Juan threw a pair of (knew new) skates (right write) over the fence.
9. Can you (sea see) if this picture is hanging (straight strait)?
10. Jai gave the (principal principle) a (piece peace) of birthday cake.

Published by Frank Schaffer Publications. Copyright protected. 50 0-7682-3225-2 *Write 4 Today*

Name **Week #20**

prewrite/brainstorm

A good way to support the topic sentence of your writing is by providing examples. Read the topic sentence in the word web below and fill in examples that support it.

The brainstorming activity should contain various ideas or words related to the topic.

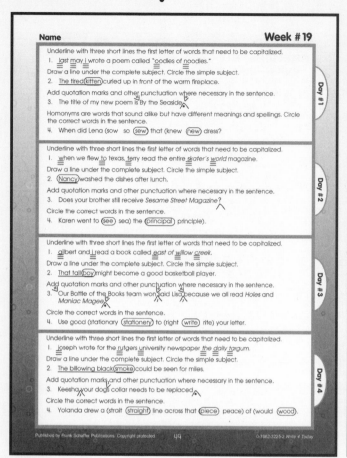

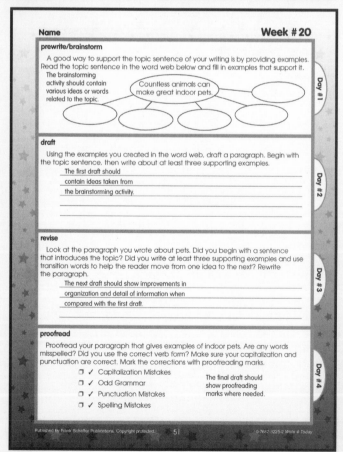

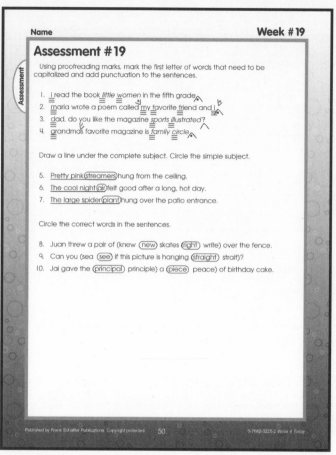

Countless animals can make great indoor pets.

Day #1

draft

Using the examples you created in the word web, draft a paragraph. Begin with the topic sentence, then write about at least three supporting examples.

The first draft should contain ideas taken from the brainstorming activity.

Day #2

revise

Look at the paragraph you wrote about pets. Did you begin with a sentence that introduces the topic? Did you write at least three supporting examples and use transition words to help the reader move from one idea to the next? Rewrite the paragraph.

The next draft should show improvements in organization and detail of information when compared with the first draft.

Day #3

proofread

Proofread your paragraph that gives examples of indoor pets. Are any words misspelled? Did you use the correct verb form? Make sure your capitalization and punctuation are correct. Mark the corrections with proofreading marks.

- ❒ ✓ Capitalization Mistakes
- ❒ ✓ Odd Grammar
- ❒ ✓ Punctuation Mistakes
- ❒ ✓ Spelling Mistakes

The final draft should show proofreading marks where needed.

Day #4

Published by Frank Schaffer Publications. Copyright protected. 51 0-7682-3225-2 *Write 4 Today*

Name **Week #20**

Assessment

Assessment #20

publish

Now it is time to publish your writing. Write your final copy on the lines below.

MAKE SURE it turns out:

- NEAT—Make sure there are no wrinkles, creases, or holes.
- CLEAN—Erase any smudges or dirty spots.
- EASY TO READ—Use your best handwriting and good spacing between words.

The content of writing samples will vary. Check to be sure that students have correctly completed all of the earlier steps in the writing process and have followed instructions for publishing their work. Use rubic on page 5 to assess.

Published by Frank Schaffer Publications. Copyright protected. 52 0-7682-3225-2 *Write 4 Today*

Answer Key

Name **Week # 21**

Use proofreading marks to correct the capitalization mistakes in the sentence.
1. on october 3, we had a birthday party!

Circle the correct verb in the sentence.
2. Tamishka (was/were) 12 years old.

Using proofreading marks, add the missing punctuation to the sentence.
3. Did you know she was that old?

Circle the correct word in the sentence.
4. (Their/There/They're) were fifteen people at the party.

Day #1

Use proofreading marks to correct the capitalization mistakes in the sentence.
1. the basketball games in march were exciting!

Circle the correct verb in the sentence.
2. The players (was/were) happy when they won the trophy.

Using proofreading marks, add the missing punctuation to the sentence.
3. The next day, they bought a case for the trophy.

Circle the correct word in the sentence.
4. (Their/There/They're) trophy is in the school gymnasium.

Day #2

Use proofreading marks to correct the capitalization mistake in the sentence.
1. Have you ever visited a different state?

Circle the correct verb in the sentence.
2. The beginning of our vacation (was/were) very busy.

Using proofreading marks, add the missing punctuation to the sentence.
3. My family visited Milwaukee, Wisconsin, and Indianapolis, Indiana.

Circle the correct verb in the sentence.
4. We like Wisconsin because (it's/its) very green and hilly!

Day #3

Use proofreading marks to correct the capitalization mistakes in the sentence.
1. my friend Sally and her cousin tabitha ate lunch together.

Circle the correct verb in the sentence.
2. Sally said the soup (was/were) delicious.

Using proofreading marks, add the missing punctuation to the sentence.
3. Sally asked her mother what she put in the soup.

Circle the correct verb in the sentence.
4. Her mother said, "(Its/It's) a secret!"

Day #4

Published by Frank Schaffer Publications. Copyright protected. 53 0-7682-3225-2 *Write 4 Today*

Name **Week # 21**

Assessment # 21

Assessment

Use proofreading marks to fix the mistakes in the ten sentences. Look for spelling, capitalization, punctuation, and grammar mistakes.

1. The Pilgrims sailed from Plymouth, England on the *Mayflower* on september 6, 1620.
2. ~~They're~~ There (sp) ~~was~~ were 102 passengers on board.
3. the beginning of the voyage ~~were~~ was pleasant, but then the ship ran into storms and high winds.
4. Beams on deck ~~was~~ were cracking and letting water leak into the ship.
5. Two adults died on the voyage, and one baby named "oceanus" ~~were~~ was born.
6. On november 9, 1620, the Mayflower neared ~~it's~~ its (sp) destination—land!
7. It ~~were~~ was where Cape Cod, Massachusetts, is now.
8. Two days later, after 66 days at sea, the ship dropped ~~it's~~ its (sp) anchor.
9. Some of the Pilgrims went ashore to check out ~~there~~ their new home.
10. Now we remember ~~there~~ their first harvest celebration on Thanksgiving Day.

Published by Frank Schaffer Publications. Copyright protected. 54 0-7682-3225-2 *Write 4 Today*

Name **Week # 22**

prewrite/brainstorm

Authors have a reason for writing: they want to entertain, inform, or persuade the reader. In persuasion, the writer wants to persuade the reader to do something or think a certain way. Begin to create a persuasive paragraph. First, list the reasons you think your father should take you to the library.

The brainstorming
activity should contain
various ideas or words
related to the topic.

Day #1

draft

Using your list of reasons to go to the library, draft a paragraph to persuade your father to take you to the library. Remember to include a topic sentence and a concluding sentence.

The first draft should
contain ideas taken from
the brainstorming activity.

Day #2

revise

Look at your rough draft. Is it persuasive? Does it have a topic sentence? Does it have points that fit your topic sentence? Did you write a concluding sentence? Rewrite your paragraph, and make your words more specific.

The next draft should show improvements in
organization and detail of information when
compared with the first draft.

Day #3

proofread

Now it's time to proofread your persuasive paragraph. Look at your final paragraph. Are all of the words spelled correctly? Did you capitalize words that need to be capitalized? Did you use the correct verbs and nouns? Proofread your paragraph.

- ❒ ✓ Capitalization Mistakes
- ❒ ✓ Odd Grammar
- ❒ ✓ Punctuation Mistakes
- ❒ ✓ Spelling Mistakes

The final draft should show proofreading marks where needed.

Day #4

Published by Frank Schaffer Publications. Copyright protected. 55 0-7682-3225-2 *Write 4 Today*

Name **Week # 22**

Assessment # 22

Assessment

publish

Now it is time to publish your writing. Write your final copy on the lines below.
MAKE SURE it turns out:
- NEAT—Make sure there are no wrinkles, creases, or holes.
- CLEAN—Erase any smudges or dirty spots.
- EASY TO READ—Use your best handwriting and good spacing between words.

The content of writing samples will vary. Check to be sure that students have correctly completed all of the earlier steps in the writing process and have followed instructions for publishing their work. Use rubic on page 5 to assess.

Published by Frank Schaffer Publications. Copyright protected. 56 0-7682-3225-2 *Write 4 Today*

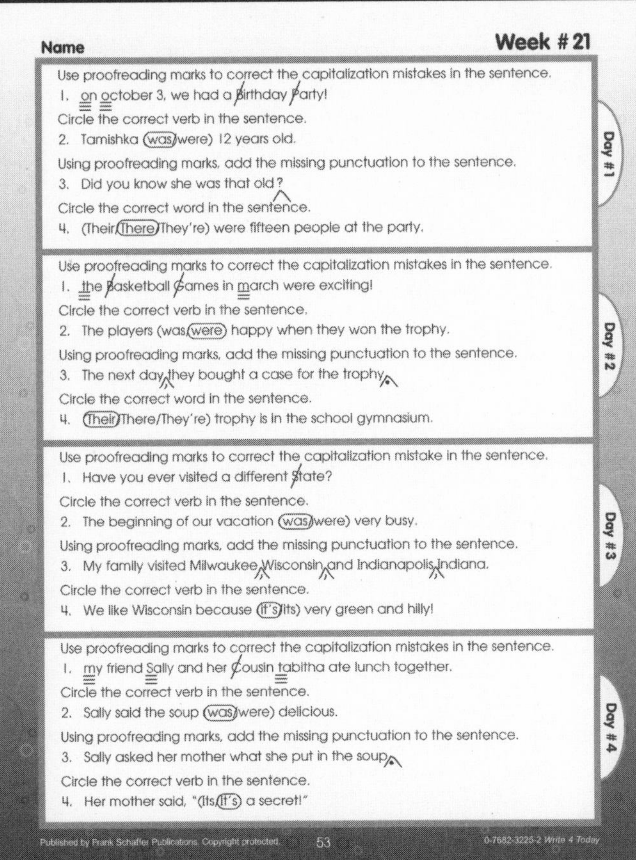

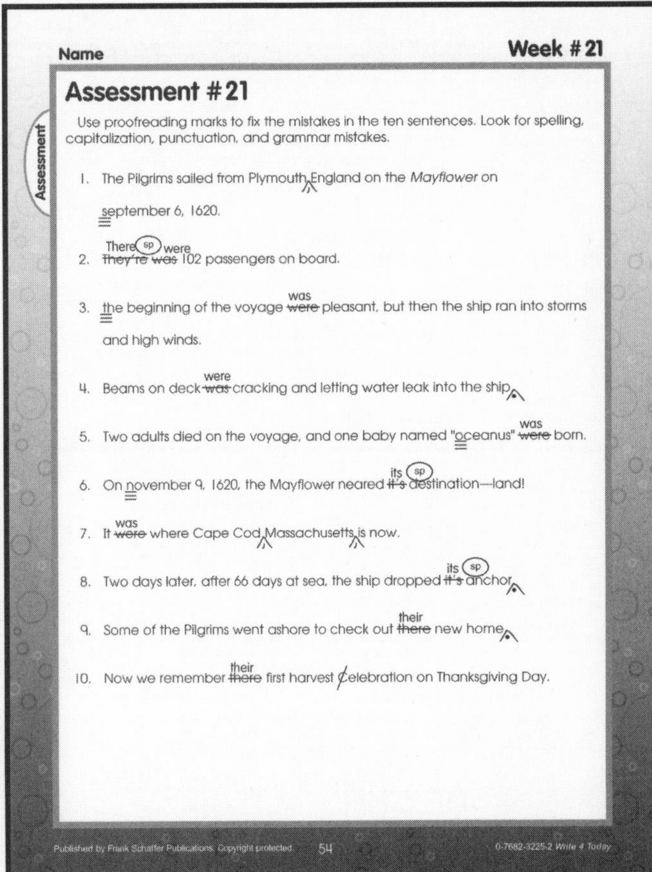

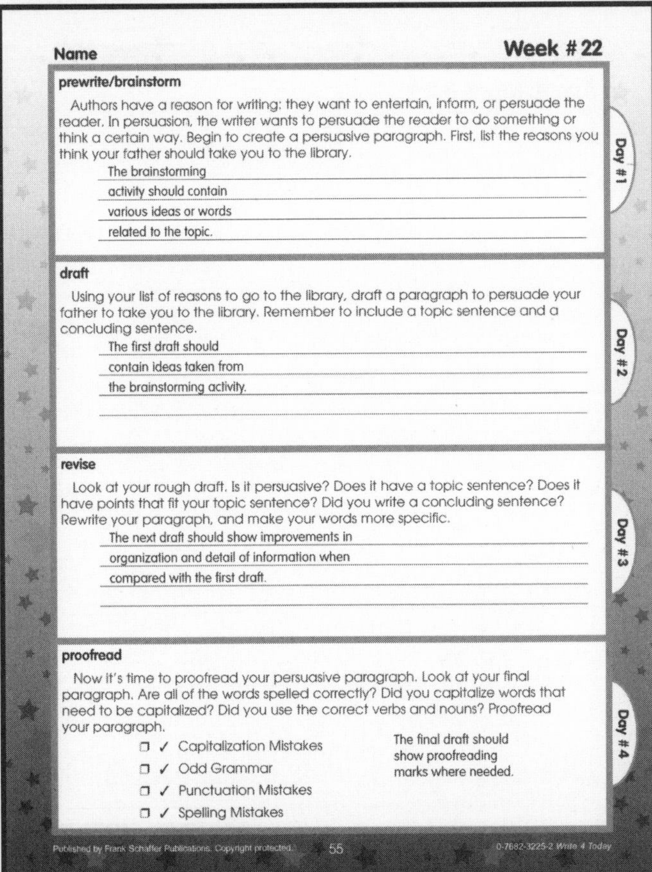

Answer Key

Name **Week # 23**

Circle the choice that shows the right capitalization.

1. a. *Harriet The Spy*
   ⓑ *Harriet the Spy*
   c. *Harriet The spy*

Write a possessive pronoun that could replace the boldfaced word.

2. His **Bryan's** dog is a basset hound.

Use a semicolon to combine the two independent clauses into a compound sentence.

3. The Olympic games originated in ancient Greece. They were held from 776 B.C. to A.D. 393.
   The Olympic games originated in ancient Greece; they were held from 776 B.C. to A.D. 393.

Cross out the incorrect reflexive pronoun. Write it correctly on the line.

4. Today I made ~~meself~~ dinner. myself

Day #1

Circle the choice that shows the right capitalization.

1. a. *Julie of The Wolves*
   b. *Julie Of The Wolves*
   ⓒ *Julie of the Wolves*

Write a possessive pronoun that could replace the boldfaced words.

2. Its **The dog's** legs are short and stocky.

Use a semicolon to combine the two independent clauses into a compound sentence.

3. The Olympic Games were held every fourth summer. The games were held at Olympia in honor of Zeus.
   The Olympic Games were held every fourth summer; the games were held at Olympia in honor of Zeus.

Cross out the incorrect reflexive pronoun. Write it correctly on the line.

4. Tim and Judy timed ~~theirself~~ running one mile. themselves

Day #2

Circle the choice that shows the right capitalization.

1. a. *The Boxcar children*
   ⓑ *The Boxcar Children*
   c. *the Boxcar children*

Write a possessive pronoun that could replace the boldfaced words.

2. Our **Kenny's and my** bedroom has bunk beds.

Use a semicolon to combine the two independent clauses into a compound sentence.

3. Women were forbidden to compete in and watch the Olympics. They held their own games called the Heraea. Women were forbidden to compete in and watch the Olympics; they held their own games called the Heraea.

Cross out the incorrect reflexive pronoun. Write it correctly on the line.

4. The coach wrote ~~hisself~~ a note to remember snacks. himself

Day #3

Circle the choice that shows the right capitalization.

1. a. *the Indian in the Cupboard*
   ⓑ *The Indian in the Cupboard*
   c. *The Indian in The Cupboard*

Write a possessive pronoun that could replace the boldfaced words.

2. theirs The picture of the sunset is **the Sandovals'**.

Use a semicolon to combine the two independent clauses into a compound sentence.

3. The women's games were held every four years. There were fewer events.
   The women's games were held every four years; there were fewer events.

Cross out the incorrect reflexive pronoun. Write it correctly on the line.

4. After we won the game, we gave ~~ourself~~ a pat on the back. ourselves

Day #4

Published by Frank Schaffer Publications. Copyright protected. 57 0-7682-3225-2 *Write 4 Today*

Name **Week # 23**

Assessment # 23

Assessment

Circle the choice that shows the right capitalization.

1. a. *the chocolate Touch*
   b. *The Chocolate touch*
   ⓒ *The Chocolate Touch*
2. ⓐ *The Case of the Muttering Mummy*
   b. *The Case of The Muttering Mummy*
   c. *The Case Of the Muttering Mummy*

For each problem, write a possessive pronoun that could replace the boldfaced words.

3. his That jacket is **Mr. Yeager's**.
4. Their **The Washingtons'** house is on Maple Avenue.
5. Our That is **Rosie's and my** teacher.

Use a semicolon to combine the two independent clauses into a compound sentence.

6. The winners were crowned with chaplets of wild olive. Their home city-states also awarded valuable gifts and privileges to the champions.
   The winners were crowned with chaplets of wild olive; their home city-states also awarded valuable gifts and privileges to the champions.
7. Discus throw was a popular event with the ancient Greeks. The champion was considered the greatest athlete.
   Discus throw was a popular event with the ancient Greeks; the champion was considered the greatest athlete.

Rewrite the sentences correctly, using the proper reflexive pronoun.

8. The boy did the dishes by hisselves.
   The boy did the dishes by himself.
9. How could we move the car by ourself?
   How could we move the car by ourselves?
10. The cats almost injured theirself when they jumped out of the tree.
    The cats almost injured themselves when they jumped out of the tree.

Published by Frank Schaffer Publications. Copyright protected. 58 0-7682-3225-2 *Write 4 Today*

Name **Week # 24**

prewrite/brainstorm

News stories contain specific facts that explain the five Ws. Pick one of the headlines below. Circle it; then make up a list that explains the five W's.

Sioux City Disc Jockey Plays Music from Helicopter / New Science Museum to Open

Who? The brainstorming
What? activity should contain
When? various ideas or words
Where? related to the topic.
Why?

Day #1

draft

Write a news story that explains the headline. Begin your story with a lead. A lead gives the important facts and is interesting, so the reader will continue to read the news story. Be sure to include your five W's.

The first draft should contain ideas taken from the brainstorming activity.

Day #2

revise

Read your news story. Did you include all five W's? Is the most important fact in the beginning of your story? Is the least important fact at the end? Did you use transition words between sentences? Rewrite the story.

The next draft should show improvements in organization and detail of information when compared with the first draft.

Day #3

proofread

Look at your news story. Are all of the words spelled correctly? Did you capitalize words that need to be capitalized? Did you use the correct verbs and nouns? Proofread your story to make sure it is correct.

- ❒ ✓ Capitalization Mistakes
- ❒ ✓ Odd Grammar
- ❒ ✓ Punctuation Mistakes
- ❒ ✓ Spelling Mistakes

The final draft should show proofreading marks where needed.

Day #4

Published by Frank Schaffer Publications. Copyright protected. 59 0-7682-3225-2 *Write 4 Today*

Name **Week # 24**

Assessment # 24

Assessment

publish

Now it is time to publish your writing. Write your final copy on the lines below.

MAKE SURE it turns out:

- NEAT—Make sure there are no wrinkles, creases, or holes.
- CLEAN—Erase any smudges or dirty spots.
- EASY TO READ—Use your best handwriting and good spacing between words.

The content of writing samples will vary. Check to be sure that students have correctly completed all of the earlier steps in the writing process and have followed instructions for publishing their work. Use rubric on page 5 to assess.

Published by Frank Schaffer Publications. Copyright protected. 60 0-7682-3225-2 *Write 4 Today*

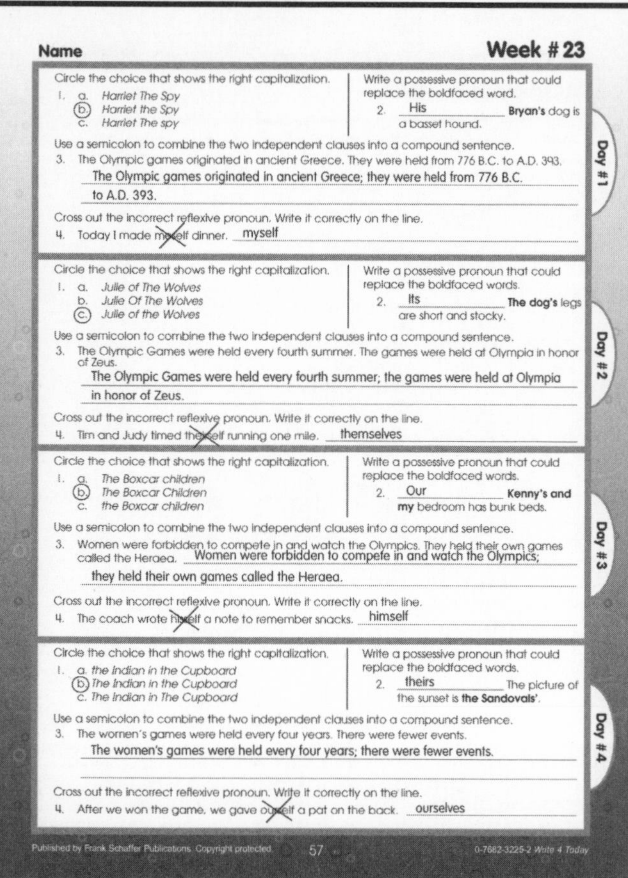

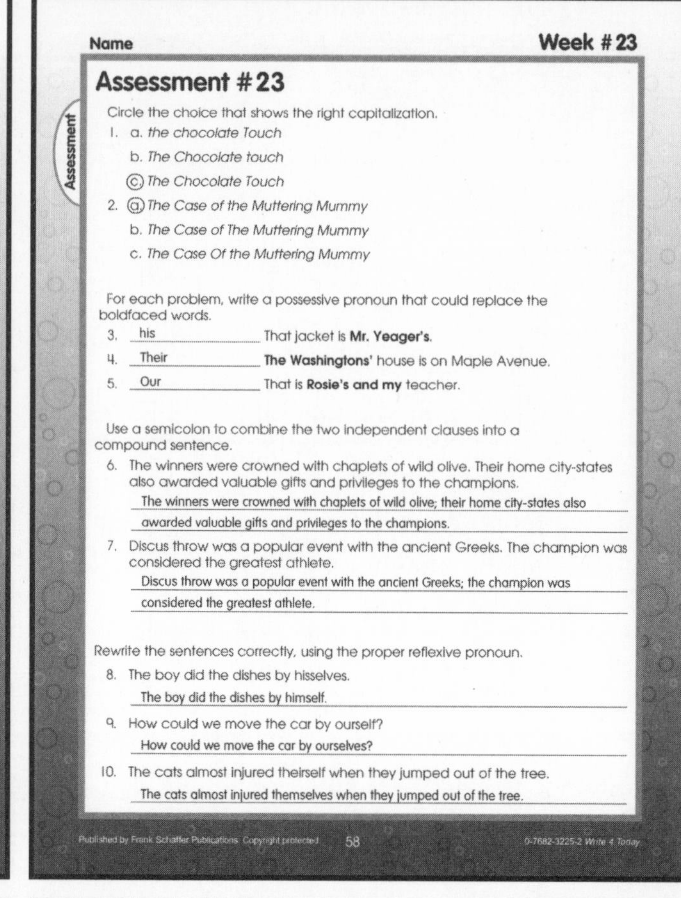

Answer Key

Name **Week #25**

Day #1

Using proofreading marks, correct the capitalization errors in the sentence.

1. Today dad and i are going to the Park.

Circle the correct word in the sentence.

2. (Its/It's) the Great Junkyard Racecar Day!

Write the missing apostrophe in the sentence. On the line, write the two words that make up the contraction or write **no contractions** if the sentence has none.

3. The fifth graders racecars had to be built using junk. no contractions

Using proofreading marks, correct the spelling error in the sentence.

4. I can't ~~weight~~ wait (sp) to see ~~whose~~ who's (sp) racing first!

Day #2

Using proofreading marks, correct the capitalization errors in the sentence.

1. the first group to race will be benjamin's Group.

Circle the correct word in the sentence.

2. My favorite teacher, Ms. Dreyden, was (their/there/they're), too.

Write the missing apostrophe in the sentence. On the line, write the two words that make up the contraction or write **no contractions** if the sentence has none.

3. Oh, no! The cars wheels fell off. Thats too bad. that is

Using proofreading marks, correct the spelling error in the sentence.

4. ~~Wich~~ Which (sp) car is your ~~favourite~~ favorite (sp)?

Day #3

Using proofreading marks, correct the capitalization errors in the sentence.

1. Wow, Mrs. nelson's Kindergarten class is at the race, too.

Circle the correct word in the sentence.

2. Isn't that (your/you're) sister over there?

Write the missing apostrophe in the sentence. On the line, write the two words that make up the contraction or write **no contractions** if the sentence has none.

3. It looks like theyre making repairs to the cars front end. they are

Using proofreading marks, correct the spelling errors in the sentence.

4. That's ~~becuz~~ because (sp) the car is going to fall ~~a part~~ apart (sp).

Day #4

Using proofreading marks, correct the capitalization errors in the sentence.

1. did you see mr. Garcia's red car in the race?

Circle the correct word in the sentence.

2. (Its/It's) the fastest car in the race.

Write the missing apostrophe in the sentence. On the line, write the two words that make up the contraction or write **no contractions** if the sentence has none.

3. Im going to build the fastest car for next years race. I am

Using proofreading marks, correct the spelling errors in the sentence.

4. Mom was ~~pleazed~~ pleased (sp) and ~~surprized~~ surprised (sp) that my sister's car stayed in one ~~peace~~ piece (sp).

Published by Frank Schaffer Publications. Copyright protected. 61 0-7682-3225-2 *Write 4 Today*

Name **Week #25**

Assessment

Assessment #25

Use proofreading marks to fix the ten mistakes in the letter below. Look for spelling, capitalization, punctuation, and grammar mistakes.

9545 Bay View Lane

Dublin, Ohio

October 22, 2004

Dear Grandma and Grandpa,

I wanted to write to tell you about Buster. He's my new puppy! Busters fur is black, and his ears are pointed. Hes always sniffing around. He likes chasing ducks at the Pond. They get so mad at him! Buster wants to play all the time, and he loves being outside. Right now, dad is giving Buster a bath…in tomato juice! Thats what we had to use ~~becuz~~ because (sp) he ~~surprized~~ surprised (sp) a skunk in our yard. Mom says the juice will take out the skunk smell. I sure hope so! Please write and tell me how ~~your~~ you're doing. I can barely ~~weight~~ wait (sp) for your visit here next month.

~~You're~~ Your grandson,

Alex

Published by Frank Schaffer Publications. Copyright protected. 62 0-7682-3225-2 *Write 4 Today*

Name **Week #26**

Day #1

prewrite/brainstorm

When you write a letter, you have a purpose: you want to share or receive information or ideas. Think of a famous person whom you admire. What would you like to tell that person? Write a list of several things you would like to tell the person in a friendly letter.

The brainstorming activity should contain various ideas or words related to the topic.

Day #2

draft

Write a short letter to the famous person. Use the ideas you listed to create a friendly message. Be sure to include the date, a greeting, and a closing with your signature.

The first draft should contain ideas taken from the brainstorming activity.

Day #3

revise

Read your draft letter. Do you begin with an introduction? Do you compliment the person? Does the letter conclude with a pleasant closing? Rewrite the letter.

The next draft should show improvements in organization and detail of information when compared with the first draft.

Day #4

proofread

Proofread your letter. Are any words misspelled? Did you use the correct verb form? Did you include the address, the date, a salutation, and a closing with your signature? Make sure your capitalization and punctuation are correct. Mark the corrections with proofreading marks.

- ❒ ✓ Capitalization Mistakes
- ❒ ✓ Odd Grammar
- ❒ ✓ Punctuation Mistakes
- ❒ ✓ Spelling Mistakes

The final draft should show proofreading marks where needed.

Published by Frank Schaffer Publications. Copyright protected. 63 0-7682-3225-2 *Write 4 Today*

Name **Week #26**

Assessment

Assessment #26

publish

Now it is time to publish your writing. Write your final copy on the lines below.

MAKE SURE it turns out:

- NEAT—Make sure there are no wrinkles, creases, or holes.
- CLEAN—Erase any smudges or dirty spots.
- EASY TO READ—Use your best handwriting and good spacing between words.

The content of writing samples will vary. Check to be sure that students have correctly completed all of the earlier steps in the writing process and have followed instructions for publishing their work. Use rubric on page 5 to assess.

Published by Frank Schaffer Publications. Copyright protected. 64 0-7682-3225-2 *Write 4 Today*

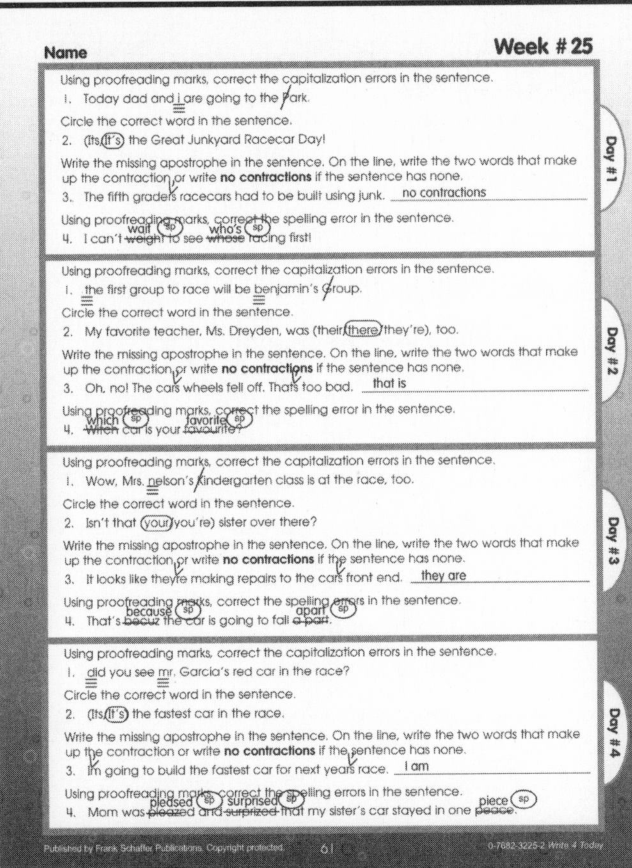

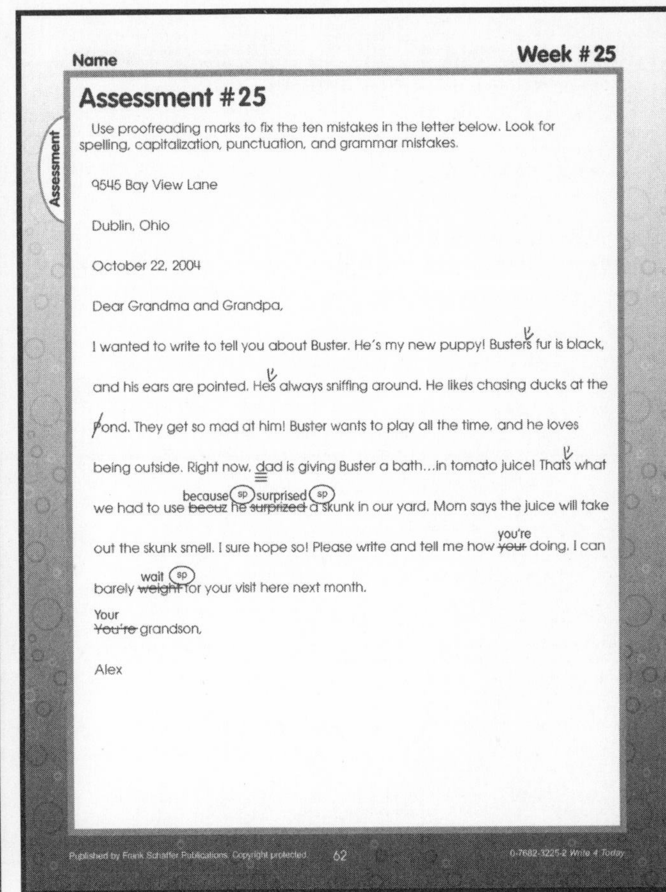

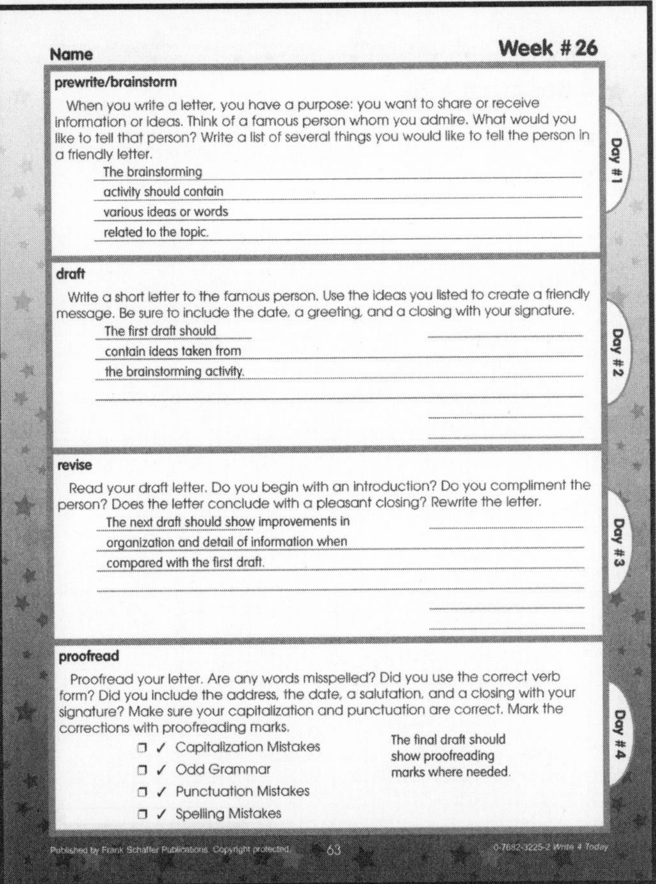

Answer Key

Name **Week # 27**

Using proofreading marks, correct the capitalization errors in the sentence.

1. my cousin will graduate from sullivan high school on june 19, 2006.

Circle the correct words in the sentence.

2. He is the (most funniest (funniest) comedian I have ever heard.

Using proofreading marks, correct the punctuation errors in the sentence.

3. Dr. Jacobs Mr. W. Allen Jr. and Father co-own that building.

Circle the correct word in the sentence.

4. Jimmy, please put the groceries over (hear, (here).

Day #1

Using proofreading marks, correct the capitalization errors in the sentence.

1. Stain Free Cleaning company transferred you to texas, right, dad?

Circle the correct words in the sentence.

2. Today's game was (more better (better) than yesterday's.

Using proofreading marks, correct the punctuation errors in the sentence.

3. Eddie that tall dark and handsome young man plays golf his brother plays tennis

Circle the correct word in the sentence.

4. ((Principal) Principle) Hillary said my brother learned a lesson.

Day #2

Using proofreading marks, correct the capitalization errors in the sentence.

1. did principal rodgers tell you that history I is now meeting in room 8?

Circle the correct words in the sentence.

2. That dress is the ((prettier) prettiest) of the two.

Using proofreading marks, correct the punctuation errors in the sentence.

3. Yes Emily I did buy tissues but I forgot the box of green tea" mother said

Circle the correct word in the sentence.

4. The ((ball) bawl) flew right through Mrs. Diego's window.

Day #3

Using proofreading marks, correct the capitalization errors in the sentence.

1. the Smith family asked for twenty-five dollars worth of gasoline.

Circle the correct words in the sentence.

2. Andrea is the (more friendly (most friendly) girl in the class.

Using proofreading marks, correct the punctuation errors in the sentence.

3. Father will I believe arrive on the 9:15 train

Circle the correct word in the sentence.

4. I didn't know Jamie went (threw, (through) the training program.

Day #4

Published by Frank Schaffer Publications. Copyright protected. 65 0-7682-3225-2 *Write 4 Today*

Name **Week # 27**

Assessment # 27

Assessment

Using proofreading marks, correct the capitalization and punctuation errors in the sentences.

1. nancy your april beauty magazine has arrived said her sister

2. yes we're going to see a play with our literature II class

3. where did you say you were going Sam?

4. the Anderson family lives near hope high school

5. Quick Printing company printed the posters flyers and cards for our sale

Circle the correct form of adjective in the sentence.

6. Who is the (louder (loudest) person in class?

7. Harry is the ((quietest) quieter) person I've ever met.

8. That old barn is the ((tallest) taller) building in the neighborhood.

Circle the correct words in the sentences.

9. My sister got a (bawl, (ball) for her fifth birthday.

10. "This summer was great!" said (Principle (Principal) Jones.

Published by Frank Schaffer Publications. Copyright protected. 66 0-7682-3225-2 *Write 4 Today*

Name **Week # 28**

prewrite/brainstorm

A movie review gives the writer's opinion of a movie. Think about a movie you have seen recently. How would you rate it? Brainstorm and make a list of your opinions about the movie. What did or didn't you like? Was it exciting or scary? Did it make you laugh or cry? What was your favorite part? Would you recommend it?

The brainstorming activity
should contain various ideas
or words related to the topic.

Day #1

draft

Write a movie review based on your list that describes your opinion of the movie. Be sure to include a topic sentence that states the movie's name and explains your opinion. Conclude your review with your recommendation.

The first draft should
contain ideas taken from
the brainstorming activity.

Day #2

revise

Read your movie review. Does the review begin in an interesting way? Will the reader understand what the movie is about? Is your opinion of the movie clear? Rewrite the review with more specific words.

The next draft should show improvements in
organization and detail of information when
compared with the first draft.

Day #3

proofread

Proofread your movie review. Are any words misspelled? Did you use the correct verb form? Did you use proper capitalization and punctuation for the movie title? Make sure all your capitalization and punctuation are correct. Mark the corrections with proofreading marks.

- ❒ ✓ Capitalization Mistakes
- ❒ ✓ Odd Grammar
- ❒ ✓ Punctuation Mistakes
- ❒ ✓ Spelling Mistakes

The final draft should show proofreading marks where needed.

Day #4

Published by Frank Schaffer Publications. Copyright protected. 67 0-7682-3225-2 *Write 4 Today*

Name **Week # 28**

Assessment # 28

Assessment

publish

Now it is time to publish your writing. Write your final copy on the lines below.

MAKE SURE it turns out:

- NEAT—Make sure there are no wrinkles, creases, or holes.
- CLEAN—Erase any smudges or dirty spots.
- EASY TO READ—Use your best handwriting and good spacing between words.

The content of writing samples will vary. Check to be sure that students have correctly completed all of the earlier steps in the writing process and have followed instructions for publishing their work. Use rubic on page 5 to assess.

Published by Frank Schaffer Publications. Copyright protected. 68 0-7682-3225-2 *Write 4 Today*

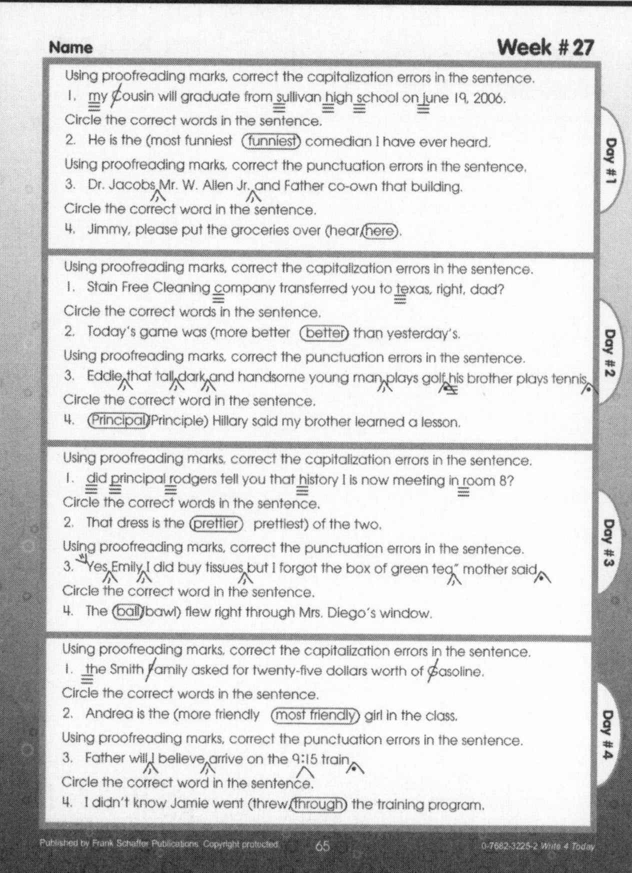

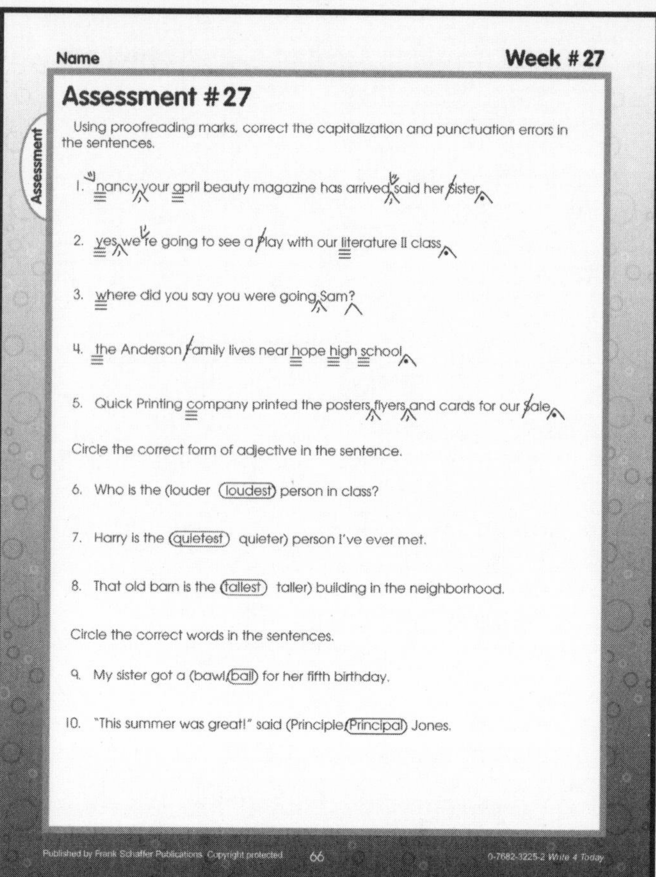

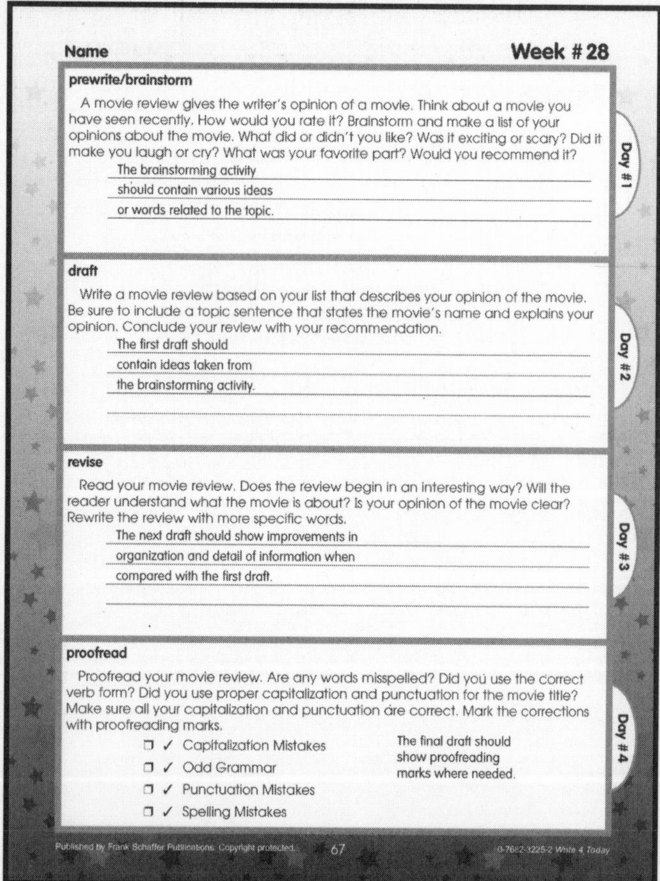

Answer Key

Name **Week #29**

Use proofreading marks to correct the capitalization error(s) in the sentence.
1. bobby smith and rachel andrews are in the same class.

Write the correct demonstrative pronoun to complete the sentence.
2. I am not wearing my glasses. Can you read __this__ note for me?

Use proofreading marks to add the missing quotation marks and comma(s).
3. The Golden Gate Bridge is one of the largest suspension bridges in the world said Mr. Yu.

Fill in the circle next to the correct verb to complete the sentence.
4. We have to ________ up two more rows of chairs.
○ sit ● set

Day #1

Use proofreading marks to correct the capitalization error(s) in the sentence.
1. Her aunt is lieutenant colonel Eleanor Cooghan.

Write the correct demonstrative pronoun to complete the sentence.
2. Mammals are warm-blooded. __That__ is a fact.

Use proofreading marks to add the missing quotation marks and comma(s).
3. Exactly how long is the bridge? asked Davida.

Fill in the circle next to the correct verb to complete the sentence.
4. The sun will ________ tonight at 7:25 p.m.
● set ○ sit

Day #2

Use proofreading marks to correct the capitalization error(s) in the sentence.
1. Do you know governor jordan of South dakota?

Write the correct demonstrative pronoun to complete the sentence.
2. The trees by the creek are huge. But __those__ across the street are small.

Use proofreading marks to add the missing quotation marks and comma(s).
3. The bridge is 8,981 feet long Mr. Yu answered and is in California.

Fill in the circle next to the correct verb to complete the sentence.
4. Logan, please ________ down.
● sit ○ set

Day #3

Use proofreading marks to correct the capitalization error(s) in the sentence.
1. Hey, dad, remember that I have Football practice after school today.

Write the correct demonstrative pronoun to complete the sentence.
2. "I like your earrings." "Thanks, my mom bought __them__ for my birthday."

Use proofreading marks to add the missing quotation marks and comma(s).
3. Mr. Yu continued The bridge has always been painted orange.

Fill in the circle next to the correct verb to complete the sentence.
4. Why don't you ________ over there?
● sit ○ set

Day #4

Published by Frank Schaffer Publications. Copyright protected. 69 0-7682-3225-2 *Write 4 Today*

Name **Week #29**

Assessment

Assessment #29

Use proofreading marks to correct the capitalization errors in the sentences.

1. the principal of their School is mr. wesley schmidt.
2. on Friday, the class is going to judge sanchez's Courtroom.

Write the correct demonstrative pronoun to complete the sentence.

3. Who donated the canned goods for the shelter? Jose donated __them__.
4. Mom picked up the racecar. "Where did you get __this__?" she asked.
5. Clayton's sister took his baseball glove. "Give me __that__!" Clayton yelled.

Use proofreading marks to add the missing quotation marks and commas.

6. Why is the bridge named Golden Gate, when its color is orange asked Marta.
7. Mr. Yu explained Actually, the term 'Golden Gate' refers to the Golden Gate Strait, the entrance to the San Francisco Bay from the Pacific Ocean.
8. Construction on the bridge began on January 5, 1933, and the bridge was opened on May 28, 1937 said Mr. Yu.

Fill in the circle next to the correct verb to complete the sentence.

9. ____ the basket of groceries on the table.
○ Sit ● Set

10. Anna usually ____ at the head of the table.
● sits ○ sets

Published by Frank Schaffer Publications. Copyright protected. 70 0-7682-3225-2 *Write 4 Today*

Name **Week #30**

prewrite/brainstorm

A paragraph that tells how things are the same or different is called a compare-and-contrast paragraph. Using the Venn diagram, write your ideas about how living in the city is different or the same as living in the country.

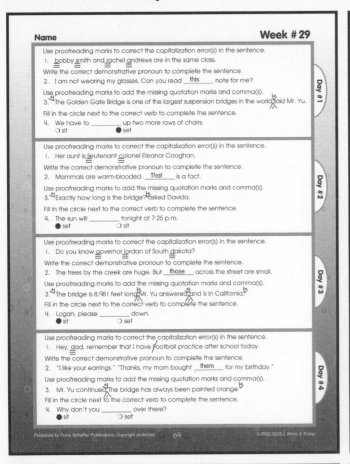

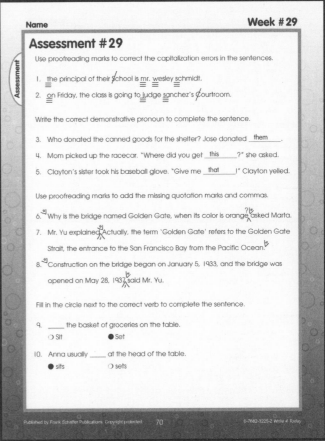

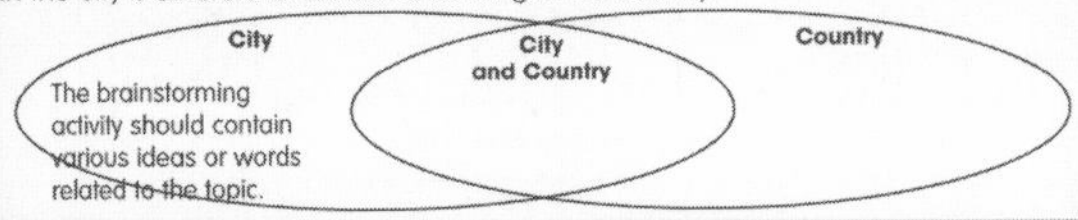

City
City and Country
Country
The brainstorming activity should contain various ideas or words related to the topic.

Day #1

draft

Use the information you wrote in the Venn diagram to write a compare-and-contrast paragraph about living in the city or country. Remember to include a topic sentence and a conclusion statement.

The first draft should contain ideas taken from the brainstorming activity.

Day #2

revise

Look at your draft. Did you begin with a topic sentence? Did you use specific words to describe similarities and differences? Did you use a conclusion sentence? Rewrite your paragraph with more specific words.

The next draft should show improvements in organization and detail of information when compared with the first draft.

Day #3

proofread

Finally, proofread your compare-and-contrast paragraph. Are all of the words spelled correctly? Did you capitalize words that need to be capitalized? Did you use the correct verbs and nouns? Make proofreading marks in your paragraph.

- ❒ ✓ Capitalization Mistakes
- ❒ ✓ Odd Grammar
- ❒ ✓ Punctuation Mistakes
- ❒ ✓ Spelling Mistakes

The final draft should show proofreading marks where needed.

Day #4

Published by Frank Schaffer Publications. Copyright protected. 71 0-7682-3225-2 *Write 4 Today*

Name **Week #30**

Assessment

Assessment #30

publish

Now it is time to publish your writing. Write your final copy on the lines below. MAKE SURE it turns out:

- NEAT—Make sure there are no wrinkles, creases, or holes.
- CLEAN—Erase any smudges or dirty spots.
- EASY TO READ—Use your best handwriting and good spacing between words.

The content of writing samples will vary. Check to be sure that students have correctly completed all of the earlier steps in the writing process and have followed instructions for publishing their work. Use rubic on page 5 to assess.

Published by Frank Schaffer Publications. Copyright protected. 72 0-7682-3225-2 *Write 4 Today*

Answer Key

Name **Week # 31**

Day #1

Fill in the circle next to the word that is capitalized correctly.

1. Cathie speaks ________ fluently.
   ❍ italian ● Italian

Write three adjectives that describe the noun.

2. kitten Answers will vary but must all be appropriate adjectives

Add the missing quotation marks around the title of the short work in the sentence.

3. Did you read "The City's Top Teacher" article in the local newspaper?

Cross out the improperly spelled reflexive pronoun in the sentence. Spell it correctly on the line.

4. Mom, I hurt ~~meself~~ while playing crack the whip. myself

Day #2

Fill in the circle next to the word that is capitalized correctly.

1. The ________ Olympians wore the brightest uniforms.
   ❍ canadian ● Canadian

Write three adjectives that describe the noun.

2. tree Answers will vary.

Add the missing quotation marks around the title of the short work in the sentence.

3. Have you heard Shel Silverstein's poem, "Screamin' Millie"?

Cross out the improperly spelled reflexive pronoun in the sentence. Spell it correctly on the line.

4. Kent bought ~~hisself~~ a pair of sunglasses. himself

Day #3

Fill in the circle next to the word that is capitalized correctly.

1. Carlos passed ________ 104, but he failed ________.
   ❍ astronomy ● Astronomy ● economics ❍ Economics

Write three adjectives that describe the noun.

2. chair Answers will vary.

Add the missing quotation marks around the title of the short work in the sentence.

3. I can't wait to get home so I can read the last chapter, "The Surprise."

Cross out the improperly spelled reflexive pronoun in the sentence. Spell it correctly on the line.

4. After the victory, the baseball team treated ~~theirself~~ to ice cream. themselves

Day #4

Fill in the circle next to the word that is capitalized correctly.

1. Lance needs to work on his ________ irregular verbs.
   ❍ spanish ● Spanish

Write three adjectives that describe the noun.

2. cactus Answers will vary.

Add the missing quotation marks around the title of the short work in the sentence.

3. Shelly is singing "The Star Spangled Banner" at the hockey game on Thursday.

Cross out the improperly spelled reflexive pronoun in the sentence. Spell it correctly on the line.

4. Justin and I gave ~~ourself~~ a second chance to run the race. ourselves

Published by Frank Schaffer Publications. Copyright protected. 73 0-7682-3225-2 *Write 4 Today*

Name **Week # 31**

Assessment

Assessment # 31

Fill in the circle next to the word that is capitalized correctly.

1. Kellie loves ______ food.
   ❍ french ● French

2. Mr. Saunders teaches ______ and ______.
   ● Journalism ❍ Journalism ❍ german ● German

3. Jason's mom is studying ______ literature.
   ● English ❍ english

Write three adjectives that describe each of the nouns.

5. cake Answers will vary.
6. dentist Answers will vary.

Add the missing quotation marks around the titles of the short works in the sentences.

6. Please give me the newspaper when you finish so I can read the article "Fleeing the Flames."
7. In the article, "Colonial Heroines," you will read the stories of four amazing women who changed the face of colonial America.
8. Did you hear Aaron Carter's song, "Another Earthquake," on the radio?

Cross out the improperly spelled reflexive pronoun in the sentence. Write it correctly on the line.

9. The girl went to the theater by ~~herselves~~. herself
10. How could you go water skiing by ~~youself~~? yourself

Published by Frank Schaffer Publications. Copyright protected. 74 0-7682-3225-2 *Write 4 Today*

Name **Week # 32**

Day #1

prewrite/brainstorm

Realistic fiction is a story that could be true but isn't. It has two main purposes: to tell an interesting story and to send an important message (theme). Use the story starter to write a realistic fiction story. Read the information, and then fill in the boxes with your ideas.

Setting: Main Characters:
Theme:
Problem: The brainstorming
Event 1: activity should contain
Event 2: various ideas or words
Event 3: related to the topic.
Solution:

Day #2

draft

Today it's time to write your realistic fiction story. Follow the story starter you made to help you to describe the problem, the three events, and the solution.

The first draft should contain ideas taken from the brainstorming activity.

Day #3

revise

Read your realistic fiction story. How could you improve it? Do you need to add more details? Do you need to rearrange the order of events? Rewrite your story. Be sure you use specific verbs and nouns to describe the characters and events.

The next draft should show improvements in organization and detail of information when compared with the first draft.

Day #4

proofread

Finally, proofread your story. Are all of the words spelled correctly? Did you capitalize words that need to be capitalized? Did you use the correct verbs and nouns? Make proofreading marks in your paragraph.

- ❒ ✓ Capitalization Mistakes
- ❒ ✓ Odd Grammar
- ❒ ✓ Punctuation Mistakes
- ❒ ✓ Spelling Mistakes

The final draft should show proofreading marks where needed.

Published by Frank Schaffer Publications. Copyright protected. 75 0-7682-3225-2 *Write 4 Today*

Name **Week # 32**

Assessment

Assessment # 32

publish

Now it is time to publish your writing. Write your final copy on the lines below.
MAKE SURE it turns out:

- NEAT—Make sure there are no wrinkles, creases, or holes.
- CLEAN—Erase any smudges or dirty spots.
- EASY TO READ—Use your best handwriting and good spacing between words.

The content of writing samples will vary. Check to be sure that students have correctly completed all of the earlier steps in the writing process and have followed instructions for publishing their work. Use rubic on page 5 to assess.

Published by Frank Schaffer Publications. Copyright protected. 76 0-7682-3225-2 *Write 4 Today*

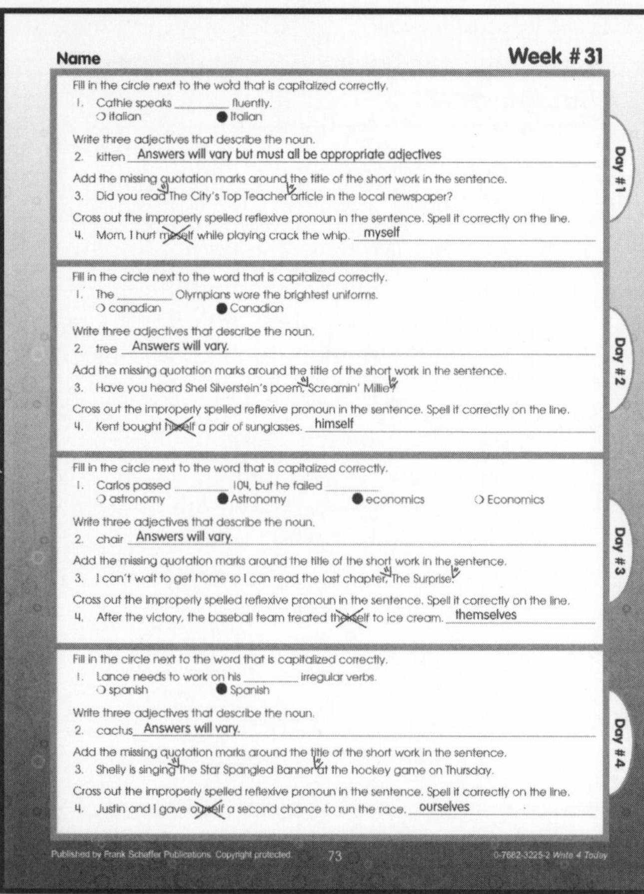

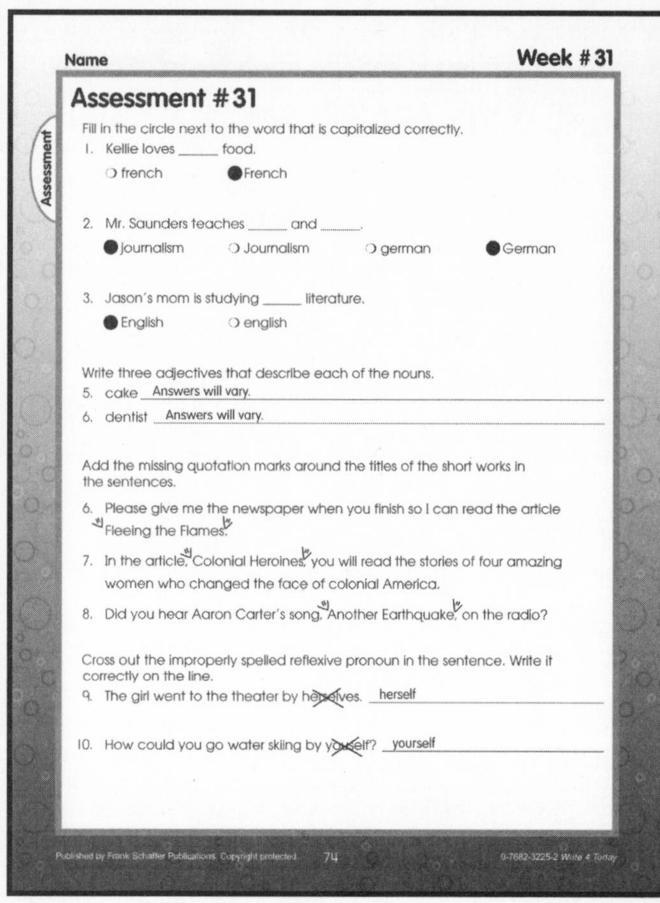

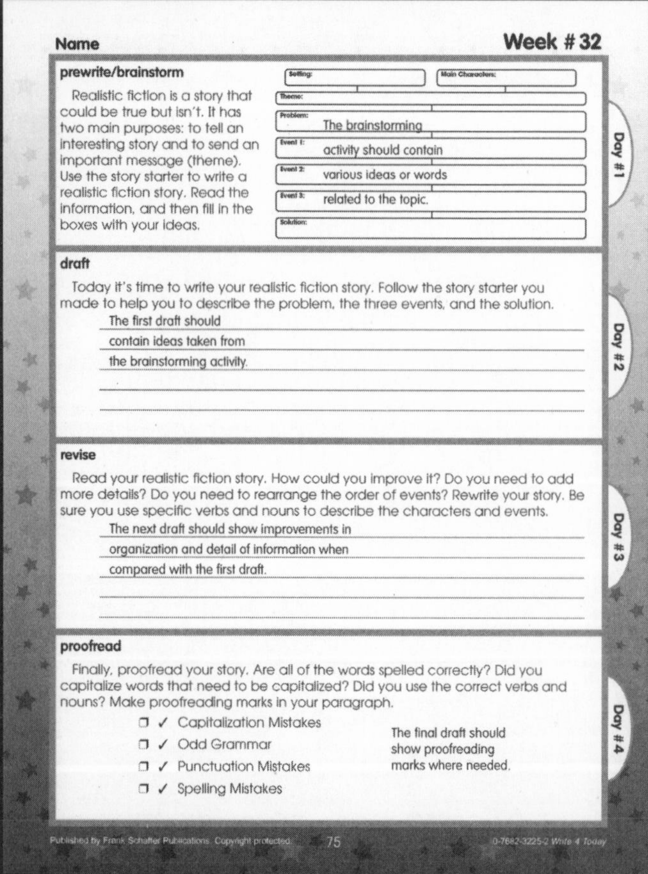

Answer Key

Name **Week #33**

Day #1

Use proofreading marks to correct the capitalization errors in the sentence.

1. Charles Lindbergh, the first person to fly nonstop from new york to paris, named his plane *the spirit of st. louis.*

Fill in the missing verb forms.

	Present Tense	Past Tense	Past Participle (use with has, had, or had)
2.	break	broke	broken
3.	bring	brought	brought

Add the missing commas to the sentences.

4. Julia, watch me throw this clock out the window. Why, Mackenzie? I want to see time fly!

Day #2

Use proofreading marks to correct the capitalization errors in the sentence.

1. The caldecott medal is awarded to the illustrator of the most distinguished children's picture book published in America.

Read the nouns in each row. Write the missing adjective and verb.

	Noun	Adjective	Adverb
2.	success	successful	successfully
3.	independence	independent	independently

Add the missing commas to the sentences.

4. Hunter, do you have a mirror? No, Tom, why? I want to see if the cat's got my tongue!

Day #3

Use proofreading marks to correct the capitalization errors in the sentence.

1. The sears tower, in chicago, illinois, has 110 stories.

Fill in the missing verb forms.

	Present Tense	Past Tense	Past Participle (use with has, had, or had)
2.	draw	drew	drawn
3.	drink	drank	drunk

Add the missing commas to the sentences.

4. Janey and Michelle, are you sick? No, we just painted our faces green!

Day #4

Use proofreading marks to correct the capitalization errors in the sentence.

1. The bill of rights is the first 10 amendments to the constitution of the united states.

Read the nouns in each row. Write the missing adjective and verb.

	Noun	Adjective	Adverb
2.	affection	affectionate	affectionately
3.	ease	easy	easily

Add the missing commas to the sentences.

4. Snort-snort! Matthew, why are you snorting like a pig? Well, Nicole, I wanted to go hog wild!

Published by Frank Schaffer Publications. Copyright protected. 77 0-7682-3225-2 *Write 4 Today*

Name **Week #33**

Assessment #33

Use proofreading marks to correct the capitalization errors in the sentence.

1. The *nina, pinta,* and *santa maria* were the three ships christopher columbus sailed on his first voyage westward.
2. Kim Dae Jung won the 2000 nobel peace prize.
3. The empire state building is taller than the john hancock center.

Fill in the missing verbs in this list of irregular past tense verbs.

	Present Tense	Past Tense	Past Participle (use with has, have, or had)
4.	get	got	gotton
	give	gave	given
5.	hide	hid	hidden
	know	knew	known
6.	speak	spoke	spoken
	take	took	taken

Add the missing commas to the sentence.

7. Will you pretend you are lightning, Fernando? OK, if you want me to.
8. Boy, that was disgusting! Don't ever make me pay through the nose again, Mrs. McCreary!

Read the nouns in each row. Write the missing adjective and adverb.

	Noun	Adjective	Adverb
9.	responsibility	responsible	responsibly
	wisdom	wise	wisely
10.	anger	angry	angrily
	silence	silent	silently

Published by Frank Schaffer Publications. Copyright protected. 78 0-7682-3225-2 *Write 4 Today*

Name **Week #34**

Day #1

prewrite/brainstorm

A business letter is more formal than a friendly letter. It is usually written to someone you do not know. Your message should be brief, clear, and to the point. You want to arrange a field trip to a local company. Use the list to plan your letter.

Who are you? (introduce yourself)

Where do you want to go? The brainstorming

What do you want to do? activity should contain

Why do you want to do this? various ideas or words

When do you want it to happen? related to the topic.

Day #2

draft

Now it's time to write your business letter. Be sure to include all of the details you wrote down on your list. On a separate sheet of paper, write a letter using the business letter form.

The first draft should contain ideas taken from the brainstorming activity.

Day #3

revise

Read over your business letter. Does the letter explain why you want to visit the local company? Does it explain the other details from your list? Is it arranged with an introduction, the body, and a closing? Rewrite the letter on another sheet of paper to make it clearer and more specific.

The next draft should show improvements in organization and detail of information when compared with the first draft.

Day #4

proofread

Today, proofread your business letter. Are all of the words spelled correctly? Did you capitalize words that need to be capitalized? Did you use the correct verbs and nouns? Make proofreading marks in your paragraph.

- ☐ ✓ Capitalization Mistakes
- ☐ ✓ Odd Grammar
- ☐ ✓ Punctuation Mistakes
- ☐ ✓ Spelling Mistakes

The final draft should show proofreading marks where needed.

Published by Frank Schaffer Publications. Copyright protected. 79 0-7682-3225-2 *Write 4 Today*

Name **Week #34**

Assessment #34

publish

Now it is time to publish your writing. Write your final copy on the lines below. MAKE SURE it turns out:

- NEAT—Make sure there are no wrinkles, creases, or holes.
- CLEAN—Erase any smudges or dirty spots.
- EASY TO READ—Use your best handwriting and good spacing between words.

The content of writing samples will vary. Check to be sure that students have correctly completed all of the earlier steps in the writing process and have followed instructions for publishing their work. Use rubic on page 5 to assess.

Published by Frank Schaffer Publications. Copyright protected. 80 0-7682-3225-2 *Write 4 Today*

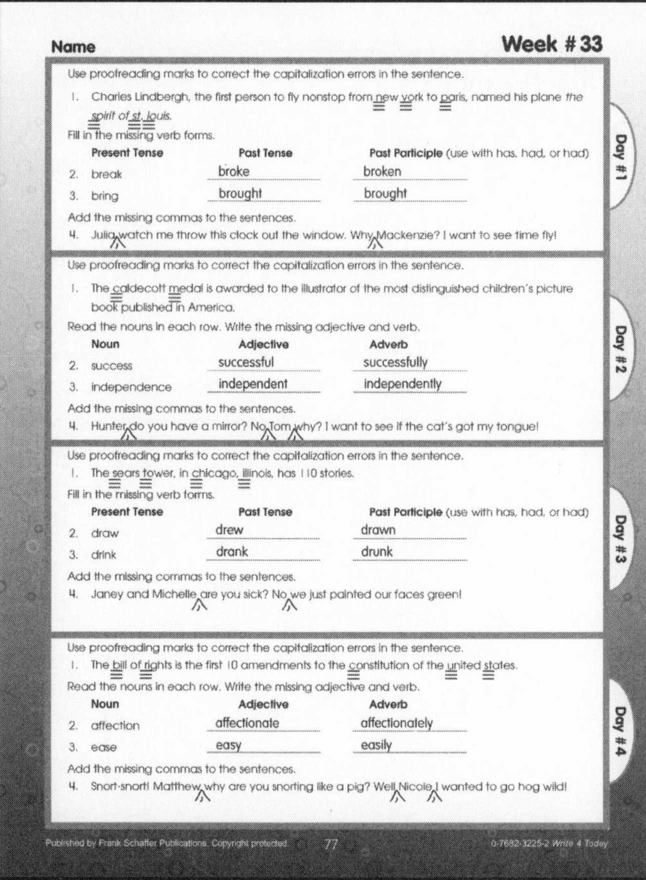

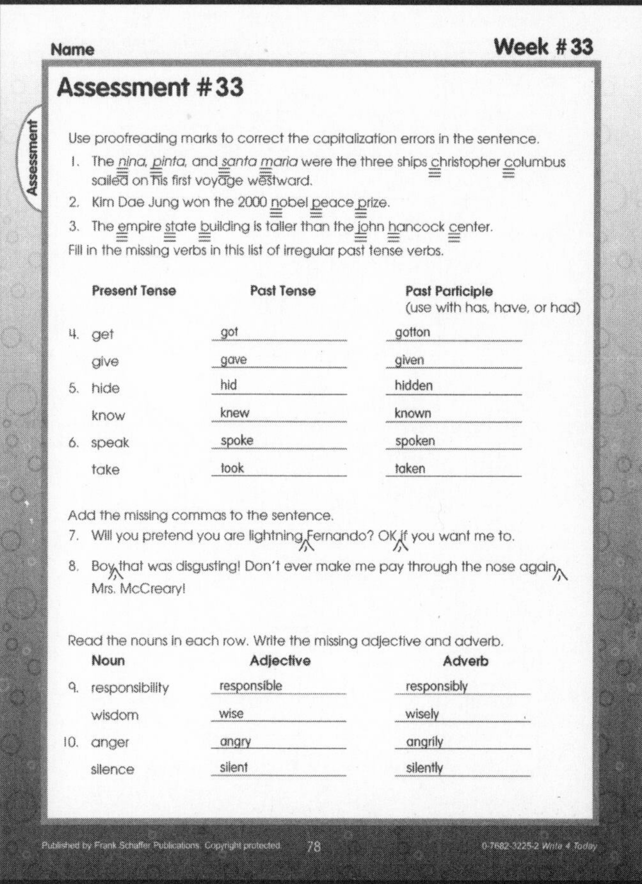

Answer Key

Name **Week #35**

Use proofreading marks to correct the capitalization.
1. I am going to visit my grandparents and my aunt eleanor.

Read the sentence. Write the correct missing word on the line.
2. Whose book is this? (Who's, Whose)

Add the missing punctuation mark and write an abbreviation to tell what kind of sentence it is: **D** (declarative), **Int** (interrogative), **Imp** (imperative), **E** (exclamatory).
3. Imp Max: Listen up, everyone.
D Mr. Chen: For math today, we are going outside to play games.

Circle the correct word to complete the sentence.
4. Mason had to (accept/except) Eli's apology.

Day #1

Use proofreading marks to correct the capitalization.
1. Did you know that dr. matthews, my dentist, is danny's mom?

Read the sentence. Write the correct missing word on the line.
2. Is that the book your reading for this month's assignment? (you're, your)

Add the missing punctuation mark and write an abbreviation to tell what kind of sentence it is: **D** (declarative), **Int** (interrogative), **Imp** (imperative), **E** (exclamatory).
3. E Class: Yay!
Int Maria: What are we going to play?

Circle the correct word to complete the sentence.
4. After a (thorough/through) search, we found the missing hamster.

Day #2

Use proofreading marks to correct the capitalization.
1. The United States has a president rather than a king or queen.

Read the sentence. Write the correct missing word on the line.
2. His aunt and uncle make him sleep in their cupboard under the stairs, while Dudley gets two bedrooms. (they're, their)

Add the missing punctuation mark and write an abbreviation to tell what kind of sentence it is: **D** (declarative), **Int** (interrogative), **Imp** (imperative), **E** (exclamatory).
3. D Mr. Chen: I don't know—you will be making up the games.
Int Kevin: How do we do that?

Circle the correct word to complete the sentence.
4. Fair-weather friends are the ones who (desert/dessert) their team when it is losing.

Day #3

Use proofreading marks to correct the capitalization.
1. Jenny wrote her report on president james madison.

Read the sentence. Write the correct missing word on the line.
2. One day a letter arrives— it's addressed to "Mr. H. Potter, The Cupboard under the Stairs." (it's, its)

Add the missing punctuation mark and write an abbreviation to tell what kind of sentence it is: **D** (declarative), **Int** (interrogative), **Imp** (imperative), **E** (exclamatory).
3. D Mr. Chen: I am giving every group a box with materials and directions.
E Julie: That sounds great!

Circle the correct word to complete the sentence.
4. I hate it when I (loose/lose) my homework!

Day #4

Name **Week #35**

Assessment

Assessment #35

Use proofreading marks to correct the capitalization.
1. During the Civil War, general robert e. lee was the leader of the Southern troops.
2. Some people believe he was America's finest general ever.

Read the sentences. Write the correct missing word on each line.
3. Harry lives with his aunt and uncle and his spoiled cousin, Dudley. They're all really mean to Harry. (They're, Their)
4. Who's the book's author? (Who's, Whose)
5. What is your favorite part so far? (you're, your)

Add the missing punctuation mark and write an abbreviation to tell what kind of sentences these are: **D** (declarative), **Int** (interrogative), **Imp** (imperative), **E** (exclamatory).
6. D Maria: There's a measuring tape, a whistle, and 10 empty two-liter bottles.
Imp Julie: Look and see if there is anything else.
7. D Yu-Chih: Here are the directions.
Imp Kevin: Read them aloud for us, Yu-Chih.
Imp Yu-Chih: Use these materials to make up a measurement relay game.
8. E Maria: Hey, this'll be fun!
Int Julie: Does anybody have an idea?

Circle the correct word to complete the sentence.
9. For the war to stop, both sides had to (accept/except) the peace plan terms.
10. I am going to lie down—please wake me when it's time for (desert/dessert).

Name **Week #36**

prewrite/brainstorm

Poetry is different from prose writing. Prose writing appears in sentences and paragraphs. Poetry appears in lines and stanzas. Brainstorm about the five senses to come up with a list of sensory words that describe water.

Water

Sight	Smell	Hearing	Taste	Touch
The brainstorming activity				
should contain various ideas				
or words related to the topic.				

Day #1

draft

Stanzas divide groups of lines and are like paragraphs. Take your ideas about water and write a poem in quatrains (four lines in each stanza). For longer poems, use another piece of paper.

The first draft should
contain ideas taken from
the brainstorming activity.

Day #2

revise

Read the poem you wrote about water. Are the lines broken into quatrains? Do you want the lines to rhyme? Look at each word. Are they the exact words that you want to use in your poem? Do the sensory words tell the reader what you think of water? Rewrite the poem to make it more specific.

The next draft should show improvements in
organization and detail of information when
compared with the first draft.

Day #3

proofread

Today, proofread your poem. Are all of the words spelled correctly? Did you capitalize words that need to be capitalized? Did you use the correct punctuation? Make proofreading marks in your poem.

- ❒ ✓ Capitalization Mistakes
- ❒ ✓ Odd Grammar
- ❒ ✓ Punctuation Mistakes
- ❒ ✓ Spelling Mistakes

The final draft should show proofreading marks where needed.

Day #4

Name **Week #36**

Assessment

Assessment #36

publish

Now it is time to publish your writing. Write your final copy on the lines below.
MAKE SURE it turns out:
- NEAT—Make sure there are no wrinkles, creases, or holes.
- CLEAN—Erase any smudges or dirty spots.
- EASY TO READ—Use your best handwriting and good spacing between words.

The content of writing samples will vary. Check to be sure that students have correctly completed all of the earlier steps in the writing process and have followed instructions for publishing their work. Use rubic on page 5 to assess.

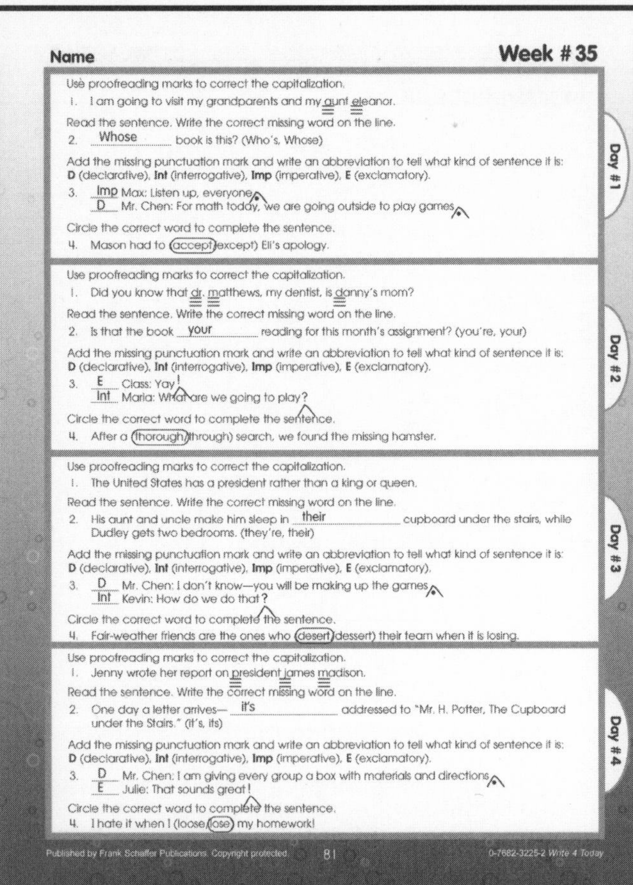

Answer Key

Name **Week # 37**

Day #1

Complete the sentence. Use correct capitalization.

1. The last movie I watched was called Answers will vary.

Rewrite the sentence twice using the past tense and the past participle of the verb.

Todd begins swimming class today.

2. (Past Tense) Todd began swimming class today.
3. (Past Participle) Todd has begun swimming class today.

Read the sentences and find the homophone errors. Use proofreading marks to correct the errors.

4. Have you ever ~~maid~~ made (sp) ice cream? ~~Its~~ It's (sp) easy ~~too~~ to (sp) do if you ~~no~~ know (sp) how.

Day #2

Complete the sentence. Use correct capitalization.

1. Some of my ancestors lived in Answers will vary.

Rewrite the sentence twice using the past tense and the past participle of the verb.

She wears shorts when it is hot.

2. (Past Tense) She wore shorts when it was hot.
3. (Past Participle) She had worn shorts when it was hot.

Read the sentences and find the homophone errors. Use proofreading marks to correct the errors.

4. My ~~Ant~~ Aunt (sp) Beth ~~tot~~ taught (sp) me how to make ~~eyes~~ ice (sp) cream. It's a ~~grate~~ great (sp) activity if ~~your board~~ you're bored (sp) or hungry.

Day #3

Complete the sentence. Use correct capitalization.

1. My favorite holiday is Answers will vary.

Rewrite the sentence twice using the past tense and the past participle of the verb.

Jamal drinks milk with breakfast.

2. (Past Tense) Jamal drank milk with breakfast.
3. (Past Participle) Jamal has drunk milk with breakfast.

Read the sentence and find the homophone errors. Use proofreading marks to correct the errors.

4. The ~~hole~~ whole (sp) project takes an ~~our~~ hour (sp) if you have the ~~write~~ right (sp) ingredients and don't need to ~~by~~ buy (sp) them.

Day #4

Complete the sentence. Use correct capitalization.

1. The person I admire most is Answers will vary.

Rewrite the sentence twice using the past tense and the past participle of the verb.

They go to school.

2. (Past Tense) They went to school.
3. (Past Participle) They have gone to school.

Read the sentence and find the homophone errors. Use proofreading marks to correct the errors.

4. ~~Bee~~ Be (sp) sure ~~ewe~~ you (sp) have milk, whipping cream, sugar, and ~~sum~~ some (sp) vanilla extract.

Name **Week # 37**

Assessment #37

Complete the sentences. Use correct capitalization.

1. My favorite book is called Answers will vary.
2. We went to Answers will vary. on vacation.
3. One of my favorite authors is Answers will vary.

Rewrite the sentence twice using the past tense and the past participle of the verb.

I see the snowstorm.

4. (Past Tense) I saw the snowstorm.
5. (Past Participle) I have seen the snowstorm.

Jennifer flies to San Francisco.

6. (Past Tense) Jennifer flew to San Fransisco.
7. (Past Participle) Jennifer has flown to San Fransisco.

Read the sentences and find the homophone errors. Use proofreading marks to correct the errors.

8. ~~Your~~ You're (sp) also going to need ~~too~~ two (sp) coffee cans, crushed ice, and a ~~hole~~ whole (sp) bag of rock salt.
9. ~~Ewe~~ You (sp) can add berries, chocolate chips, or candy to the ice cream, ~~two.~~ too (sp)
10. With ~~sum~~ some (sp) ordinary ingredients and my ~~ant's~~ aunt's (sp) recipe, you ~~to~~ too (sp) can make your own ice cream.

Name **Week # 38**

Day #1

prewrite/brainstorm

Dialogue is the words spoken by characters in a story. Dialogue should be realistic. For example, a young child uses different words and phrases than an adult does. Think about the following situation and brainstorm about things the characters might say to each other. Make a list of your ideas on a separate sheet of paper.

A first grader asking for help from an older brother.

The brainstorming activity should contain various ideas or words related to the topic.

Day #2

draft

Write a conversation between the first grader and the older brother. Use quotation marks, commas, and end punctuation correctly.

The first draft should contain ideas taken from the brainstorming activity.

Day #3

revise

Read over your conversation. Is it clear who is saying what? Do the words that the characters use fit their ages? Are the words written as if the characters were actually saying the words? Revise the conversation.

The next draft should show improvements in organization and detail of information when compared with the first draft.

Day #4

proofread

Now it's time to proofread the conversation. Are all of the words spelled correctly? Did you capitalize words that need to be capitalized? Did you use the correct quotation marks, commas, and other punctuation? Mark corrections with proofreading marks.

- ❒ ✓ Capitalization Mistakes
- ❒ ✓ Odd Grammar
- ❒ ✓ Punctuation Mistakes
- ❒ ✓ Spelling Mistakes

The final draft should show proofreading marks where needed.

Name **Week # 38**

Assessment #38

publish

Now it is time to publish your writing. Write your final copy on the lines below.
MAKE SURE it turns out:

- NEAT—Make sure there are no wrinkles, creases, or holes.
- CLEAN—Erase any smudges or dirty spots.
- EASY TO READ—Use your best handwriting and good spacing between words.

The content of writing samples will vary. Check to be sure that students have correctly completed all of the earlier steps in the writing process and have followed instructions for publishing their work. Use rubric on page 5 to assess.

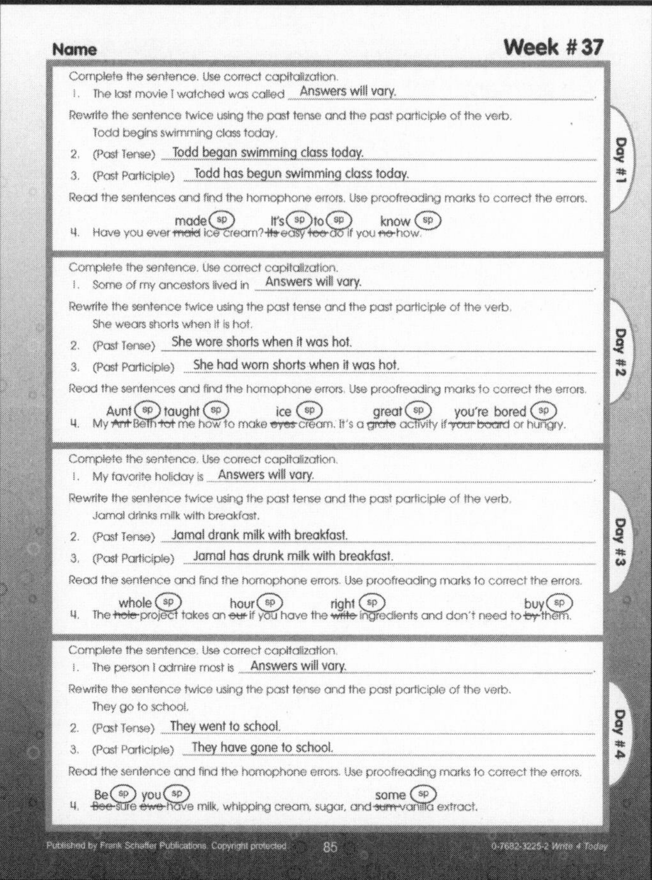

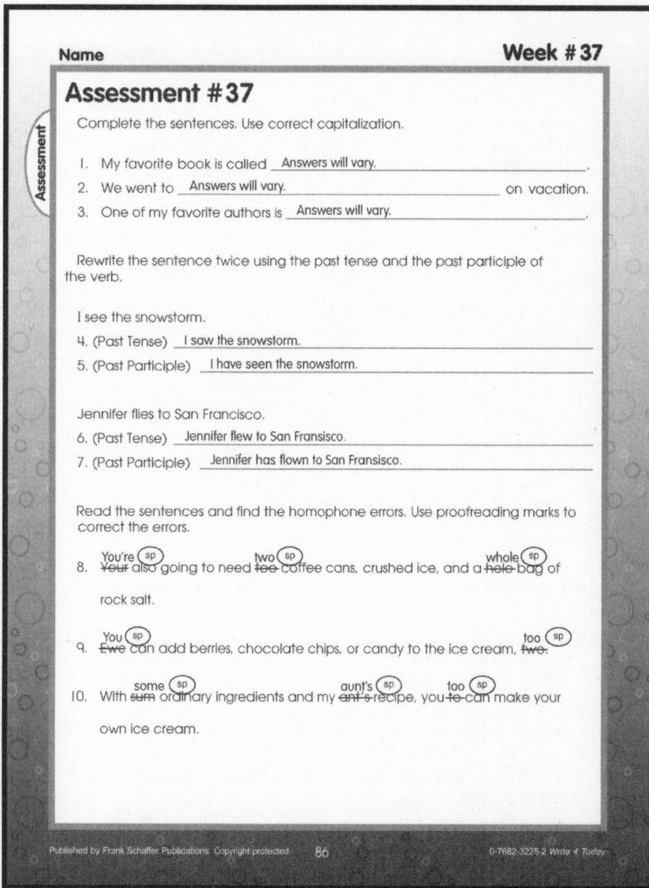

Answer Key

Name **Week #39**

Day #1

Use proofreading marks to correct the capitalization errors in the sentence.
1. Many types of cars, like the pacer, edsel, and gremlin, are no longer made.

Write *declarative, imperative, exclamatory,* or *interrogative* before the sentence. Add end punctuation and add periods after initials and abbreviations.
2. interrogative Where are you going on your next vacation?

Write the contractions for each pair of words.
3. you are you're
does not doesn't

Write the plural for these nouns.
4. march marches
boy boys

Day #2

Use proofreading marks to correct the capitalization errors in the sentence.
1. If you could attend a major sporting event, would you rather go to the super bowl, the stanley cup playoffs, or the kentucky derby?

Write *declarative, imperative, exclamatory,* or *interrogative* before the sentence. Add end punctuation and add periods after initials and abbreviations.
2. declarative Dr J C Brown taught at Harvard

Write the contractions for each pair of words.
3. he is he's
could not couldn't

Write the plural for these nouns.
4. church churches
agency agencies

Day #3

Use proofreading marks to correct the capitalization errors in the sentence.
1. josh belongs to the boy scouts, pitches in little league, and was elected president of the lakeside stamp club last march.

Write *declarative, imperative, exclamatory,* or *interrogative* before the sentence. Add end punctuation and add periods after initials and abbreviations.
2. imperative Sgt Burns, go to the colonel's office

Write the contractions for each pair of words.
3. they were they're
was not wasn't

Write the plural for these nouns.
4. sketch sketches
jelly jellies

Day #4

Use proofreading marks to correct the capitalization errors in the sentence.
1. independence day, presidents day, memorial day, labor day, and christmas are all holidays.

Write *declarative, imperative, exclamatory,* or *interrogative* before the sentence. Add end punctuation and add periods after initials and abbreviations.
2. imperative Always be on time

Write the contractions for each pair of words.
3. you have you've
is not isn't

Write the plural for these nouns.
4.. fox foxes
family families

Name **Week #39**

Assessment #39

Use proofreading marks to correct the capitalization errors in the sentence.

1. The students were given a choice of writing about the revolutionary war, the reconstruction era, the industrial revolution, or the civil war as topics for their history reports.

2. In january, i got to go on a tour of the general electric headquarters in new york city.

Write *declarative, imperative, exclamatory,* or *interrogative* before each sentence. Add end punctuation and add periods after initials and abbreviations.
3. imperative Don't slam the door when you leave
4. declarative Grandmother asked me to help her on Tuesday
5. interrogative Was U S Grant a popular president?

Write the contractions for each pair of words.

6. you are you're	they were they're
7. does not doesn't	could not couldn't
8. you have you've	he is he's

Write the plural for these nouns.

9. march marches	church churches
10. agency agencies	family families

Name **Week #40**

Day #1

prewrite/brainstorm

When fiction writers select a narrator to tell the story, they choose a point of view. First-person narrators use I/me/my pronouns. Third-person narrators use he/she or the character's name. On the lines below, list some things that happen when you take your pet to the veterinarian.

The brainstorming activity should contain various ideas or words related to the topic.

Day #2

draft

Using the first-person point of view, write a short paragraph about taking a pet to the veterinarian. Next, write the same information in another short paragraph using third-person narration.

The first draft should contain ideas taken from the brainstorming activity.

Day #3

revise

Today, revise your two paragraphs told from two points of view. Is the point of view clear in each paragraph? How does the reader know what the point of view is? Rewrite each paragraph, using more specific nouns and verbs.

The next draft should show improvements in organization and detail of information when compared with the first draft.

Day #4

proofread

Now it's time to proofread the two paragraphs. Are all of the words spelled correctly? Did you capitalize words that need to be capitalized? Did you use correct punctuation? Make proofreading marks in your paragraph.

- ❒ ✓ Capitalization Mistakes
- ❒ ✓ Odd Grammar
- ❒ ✓ Punctuation Mistakes
- ❒ ✓ Spelling Mistakes

The final draft should show proofreading marks where needed.

Name **Week #40**

Assessment #40

publish

Now it is time to publish your writing. Write your final copy on the lines below.
MAKE SURE it turns out:
- NEAT—Make sure there are no wrinkles, creases, or holes.
- CLEAN—Erase any smudges or dirty spots.
- EASY TO READ—Use your best handwriting and good spacing between words.

The content of writing samples will vary. Check to be sure that students have correctly completed all of the earlier steps in the writing process and have followed instructions for publishing their work. Use rubic on page 5 to assess.

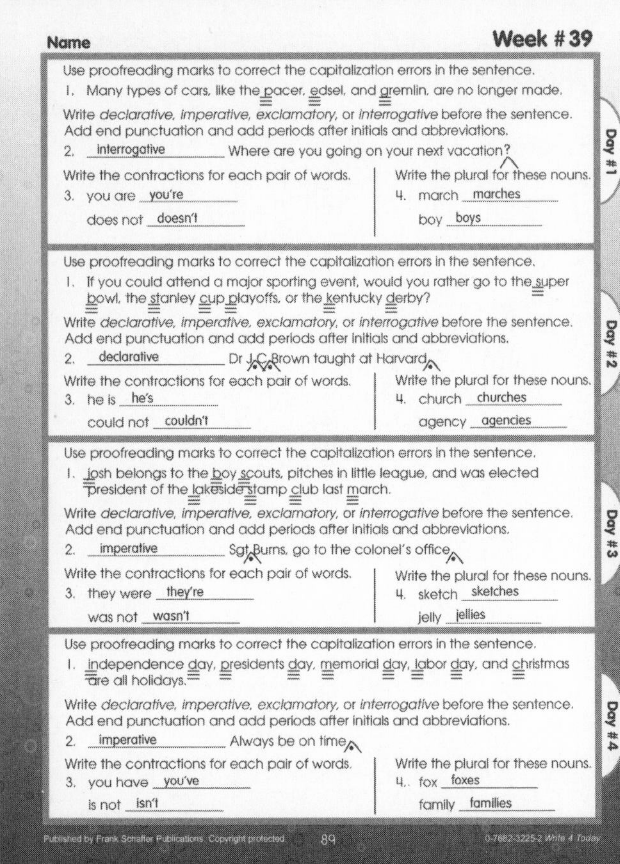